# ADVANCED JUJITSU

by George Kirby

## The Science Behind the Gentle Art

# ADVANCED JUJITSU

by George Kirby

## The Science Behind the Gentle Art

Edited by Raymond Horwitz,
Jeannine Santiago and Jon Thibault

Photos by Rick Hustead

Graphic Design by John Bodine


Printed in the United States of America
Library of Congress Control Number: 2006923807
ISBN-10: 0-89750-152-7
ISBN-13: 978-0-89750-152-1

*First Printing 2006*

**WARNING**

This book is presented only as a means of preserving a unique aspect of the heritage of the martial arts. Neither Ohara Publications nor the author make any representation, warranty or guarantee that the techniques described or illustrated in this book will be safe or effective in any self-defense situation or otherwise. You may be injured if you apply or train in the techniques illustrated in this book and neither Ohara Publications nor the author is responsible for any such injury that may result. It is essential that you consult a physician regarding whether or not to attempt any technique described in this book. Specific self-defense responses illustrated in this book may not be justified in any particular situation in view of all of the circumstances or under applicable federal, state or local law. Neither Ohara Publications nor the author make any representation or warranty regarding the legality or appropriateness of any technique mentioned in this book.

# ACKNOWLEDGMENTS

Writing a technical book is rarely a solo effort. It takes a lot of qualified people to assist in writing a well-rounded book. In the case of *Advanced Jujitsu: The Science Behind the Gentle Art*, it took a number of martial artists and non-martial artists to help me put this book together for your enjoyment. I consider myself fortunate to know people of such varied expertise who were willing to help me develop the material for this book.

David Carletta, chiropractor and a former *jujitsu* student of mine, whose invaluable knowledge helped resolve some of the issues surrounding joint hierarchies and the root joint-humanoid joint clarification. Dr. Carletta also suggested a number of relevant reading resources.

Nadine Stegg, New York state certified physical therapist, who also assisted me in my search for suitable references dealing with joint hierarchy.

Ron Sekulich, Mark Jordan and Mark Tucker (all *sensei*), who unselfishly served as *uke* for this book, provided some technical advice during the photo shoot and have stood by my side for many years.

- Ron Sekulich, fourth-degree black belt in *budoshin* jujitsu and head instructor of the City of Burbank Parks & Recreation Dept. jujitsu program at the Verdugo Recreation Center, has been a student of mine since 1989. He has been teaching since 1995. Ron and Mark Jordan both officially took over the Burbank Parks program in 1996.

- Mark Jordan, fourth-degree black belt in budoshin jujitsu, is uniquely fortunate to be teaching jujitsu at the Harvard Westlake School in Studio City and in Westlake, California, since 1998 as a physical education teacher. Mark started his training with me in 1988 as a white belt, achieved *shodan* in 1993, and started teaching at the Verdugo Recreation Center Dojo in 1994.

- Marc Tucker, fourth-degree black belt in budoshin jujitsu, has been co-instructing with me at the City of Santa Clarita's Parks, Recreation and Community Services Dept.'s budoshin jujitsu program since 1997. Marc is a financial consultant with Financial West Group in Tarzana, California. From 1964 to 1970, sensei Tucker was a student of Jack Seki (who was my instructor as well).

Marc Kolodziejczyk, first-degree black belt in budoshin jujitsu and professional artist, who helped me with some of the artwork in this book. Marc is also one of the assistant instructors in the Santa Clarita *dojo*.

John Wilson, avid backpacker and photographer, who, 30 years ago, took the time to teach me some of the body-awareness techniques presented in this book.

Scott Shaver, another avid backpacker and professional photographer who was a student of mine at Olive Vista Jr. High School 30 years ago, turned me onto backpacking and facilitated my meeting John Wilson. I reconnected with Scott in fall 2005 through an Internet search. He was able to help me locate John Wilson. Thank you, Scott, for bringing back a lot of positive memories.

Special thanks to the Black Belt Communications staff, especially Robert Young, Raymond Horwitz and Jon Thibault, who had faith in my ability to write such a technically oriented book, the patience necessary to keep me on track, and the know-how to craft this book into its final form.

# DEDICATION

William D. Fromm
***1935 – 2003***

I first met Bill in 1967, when I was a new *jujitsu* student at the YMCA in Burbank, California. He was a brown belt and I was a white belt. There really was no relationship at that time beyond his being the assistant *sensei* at the YMCA. Because I had the time and wanted more instruction, I started taking classes three additional nights per week from the chief sensei, Jack Seki, and I got to know Bill better. Bill's sensei stopped teaching at the YMCA, so Seki told Bill and me to co-instruct.

The program soon got so big that we had a six-month waiting list. Bill and I got to know each other very well. He was the planning director for the city of Burbank, and although our political views often clashed, we trusted each other's judgment and he was a great person to work with. I think this dynamic made the Burbank jujitsu program work as well as it did and made our friendship more cohesive.

After a few years, Bill moved to Towson, Maryland, to become the planning director for that city. His leaving was a real loss to me, but he

Photo courtesy of George Kirby

Bill Fromm (left), *sensei* Jack Seki and George Kirby in 1970.

quickly started a jujitsu program at the Towson YMCA that still exists today. Seki suggested that Bill and I create a federation. After quite a bit of discussion, we established the American Ju-Jitsu Association (AJA). In retrospect, this seems to have been Seki's way of making sure both of us stayed in contact with each other.

Our close friendship continued until Bill's passing in July 2003. We went through familial trials and joys together. We went through political machinations as the AJA grew. Even after Bill moved to Kentucky, retiring from both public service and from teaching jujitsu, we continued to write and talk to each other on a regular basis. We even dealt with the aches and pains of being "seniors" together, but we were able to laugh at our problems and make fun of our new limitations. Life does go on.

Early in 2003, Bill informed me that he had been diagnosed with Parkinson's disease. On Monday, July 14, 2003, Bill's wife Aldeen called me to let me know that he had suddenly died. It was an absolute shock, and I'm still dealing with it to this day.

Bill's friendship and support was a very important part of my life. He was the one person I could bounce my thoughts off of without fear of criticism or mockery. He was always straight with me. I didn't always agree with what he said, but I knew he was being honest and sincere, and I could trust his judgment. He was a true friend. He was my rock.

Though I shall truly miss him, I have a lot of fond memories of Bill—and those will win out in the end. I know he's on the great *tatami* in the sky, where he should be.

~·~

I would like to dedicate this book to you, Bill. You dedicated your life to the art and helped me become who I am today. I can only hope that I can have the same positive influence and impact on someone else's life.

*—George Kirby*

# ABOUT THE AUTHOR

In 1968, George Kirby had no idea where martial arts training would take him. He was a first-degree brown belt (*ikkyu*) in *sensei* Jack "Sanzo" Seki's *jujistu* ("gentle art") program at Los Angeles Valley College. It was a class he took purely for relaxation from the stress of studying for his Master of Arts degree exams at California State University, Los Angeles.

A twist of fate landed Kirby in a very interesting predicament when Seki went up to Kirby and said: "Georgie, I want you and Bill Fromm (another brown belt) to take over the Burbank YMCA program. The instructor has to leave."

Kirby responded: "Sensei, I'm only a brown belt. How can I teach a class?"

"Bill knows more techniques, but you're a [school] teacher, so you can both teach the class."

Continuing his protest, Kirby responded, "But sensei, we're only brown belts."

Seki put an end to the debate by declaring: "Now you're both black belts. Act like it."

And thus Kirby's life as a sensei (teacher) began. Sensei Seki, according to Kirby, never asked his students to do something. He simply told them. Years later, Seki would tell Kirby he had faith in his abilities to perform well as a sensei. It appears that Seki was correct—Kirby has been a sensei for 39 years.

Kirby took on his teaching position at the Burbank YMCA in 1968. The program moved to the City of Burbank Parks and Recreation Department in 1974, where it continues to this day. That year, he met his future wife, Adel, who is also a school teacher. They married in 1976 and were blessed in 1986 with their daughter, Kimberly, who Kirby says, "is growing up to be a caring and well-educated young lady."

Kirby left the Burbank Parks program in 1996 to start a new jujitsu program with the City of Santa Clarita Parks and Recreation Department, where he still teaches jujitsu classes on a weekly basis. During the late 1970s to 1983, Kirby taught social studies and jujitsu (as an elective class or for physical education credit) at Olive Vista Jr. High School in Sylmar, California. His jujitsu class was overwhelmingly popular, growing to four classes out of his five-period day by the time he left the school in January 1983.

Among Kirby's most lasting contributions to the martial arts has been the American Ju-Jitsu Association (AJA), which he formed with Bill Fromm at the suggestion of Seki. By the late 1970s, the AJA had become a national governing body of jujitsu and, under the IRS code 501(c)(3), established itself as an amateur athletic association. The organization has continued to grow in size and influence over the years, handling a number of *ryu* (styles) of jujitsu and becoming an internationally-recognized governing body. Although he initially served as president of the AJA, the administrative duties of the organization have been delegated to others in recent years. Kirby now serves as chairman of its board of directors. In addition, he is also the founder and chairman of the board of directors of the Budoshin Ju-Jitsu Dojo, Inc., a non-profit educational foundation, and the Budoshin Ju-Jitsu Yudanshakai, a research and educational foundation.

In 1994, Kirby was one of several nationally recognized martial artists to be selected by the Los Angeles Police Department (LAPD) to develop a new arrest-and-control program following the Rodney King controversy. That core of marital artists became known as the Civilian Martial Arts Advisory Panel (CMAAP). As a defensive tactics consultant for the LAPD, Kirby continued to serve law enforcement through the CMAAP, dealing with issues involving officer safety in the areas of arrest and control. During that time, he met top martial artists from other arts, working with them for a common purpose. In 1998, the City of Los Angeles awarded all the CMAAP members Certificates of Appreciation for their commitment to developing one of the nation's top arrest-and-control training programs.

Amidst the flurry of all this prestigious public work, writing had always been an aspiration of this martial arts expert. Although several of his articles had been published in *Black Belt* in the late 1970s and early 1980s, writing a book on jujitsu had been somewhat of a remote dream. However, all that changed in 1982 at the Ohara Publications/Black Belt Communications office. Kirby was conversing with Gregory Lee, a former Ohara/Black Belt editor, when he ran into then-assistant publisher Geri Simon. Lee introduced the two of them, at which point Simon mentioned that she was considering a book on jujitsu and asked if Kirby was interested in submitting a proposal. Of course, he was and did—and the rest is history.

Since that day of opportunity, Kirby has written four books before this one for Black Belt Communications: *Jujitsu: Basic Techniques of the Gentle Art* (1983), *Jujitsu: Intermediate Techniques of the Gentle Art* (1985), *Jutte: Power of Ten Hands Weapon* (1987) and *Jujitsu Nerve Techiques: The Invisible Weapon of Self-Defense* (2001). He has also self-published *Budoshin*

*Ju-Jitsu: The Big Book*, which is now in its fifth edition. Kirby has also produced a VHS and DVD series titled *Budoshin Ju-Jitsu Black Belt Home Study Course* for Panther Productions. The videos correlate with the concepts presented in his books, creating what Kirby calls "a tremendously useful instructional resource for the serious martial artist."

Kirby has also been involved with a number of national and international organizations. He is currently a member of the World Grandmaster Council, Dai Nippon Seibukan Budo/Bugei-kai (All-Japan Martial Arts and Ways Association), the World Martial Arts Accreditation Council, International Jujitsu Federation Nippon Seibukan and the American Society for Law-Enforcement Training, among others.

In 1997, Kirby received the title of *hanshi* (master). And in 2000, he was promoted to *judan* (10th-dan black belt) in jujitsu. This distinguished career in the martial arts began as an effort to relax during intensive master's degree studies (which paid off when Kirby received his Master's in Social Science in 1969). It's led to a career as a jujitsu instructor, martial arts council member, and published author in addition to his academic career. Since 1995, he has been the Social Science Department Chairperson at Ulysses S. Grant High School in Van Nuys, California, where he teaches Honors Economics, Honors Government and Advanced Placement Government.

In connecting his academic and martial arts careers, Kirby says: "Teaching jujitsu and social sciences in public school is still fun and enjoyable because the students and the intrinsic rewards of teaching have made it so. It is an honor to be a teacher, a sensei."

# FOREWORD

I have had the pleasure of knowing George Kirby since the early 1980s. We have worked together at martial arts camps and as representatives of the *jujitsu* organizations to which we belong. I have found him to be a very dedicated and professional martial artist who has committed his adult life to helping others learn jujitsu. It is an honor to write a foreword for this book.

*Advanced Jujitsu: The Science Behind the Gentle Art* is the fifth book he has written for Black Belt Communications. In this book, George continues his tradition of presenting martial arts theories in a clear manner so that other martial artists can learn. Like his other books, many of the ideas presented can be applied to martial arts other than jujitsu.

This book concentrates on meditation and the physics of body movement in the martial arts. Professor Kirby also shows how these two topics can be brought together to help all martial artists grow in their own arts.

Take your time in reading this book. Think about what you are reading. This book may prompt you to rethink your art and how it works. But most importantly, it has many good ideas that can help you become a better martial artist and a more fulfilled person.

—*Professor Wally Jay*

# PREFACE

Most martial arts books present a whole series of techniques. They start you at point "A" and move you toward a quantitative learning objective: "x" quantity and variety of techniques, requirements for certain belt levels, etc. They have a common goal: to increase your knowledge, ability and skill level within a particular martial art. In short, they teach techniques.

This book is different.

It doesn't teach techniques.

It teaches *technique* ... how to do what you do better, why things work the way they do, and elements common within many martial arts.

All of the techniques shown in this book are fairly basic movements from the martial art of *jujitsu*. None of them are new. They are described in much greater detail in my other books: *Jujitsu: Basic Techniques of the Gentle Art* (Ohara, 1983), *Jujitsu: Intermediate Techniques of the Gentle Art* (Ohara, 1985) and *Jujitsu Nerve Techniques: The Invisible Weapon of Self-Defense* (Ohara, 2001). My Panther/Century DVD instructional series, *Budoshin Jujitsu Black Belt Home Study Course*, (available at http://www.budoshin.com or from Century Martial Arts) also discusses these techniques in detail. However, because jujitsu is a parent art, the movements, theory and application most surely can be applied to your art as well.

As you study this book, find its relationship to what you know. This will not be a difficult undertaking. Apply the content of this book to what you know. It will make you a better martial artist and a better person. Accept the commonalities that will help you better understand your martial art, the simplicity of how it works as it does, and the inherent similarities between the arts.

If understanding your martial art is your goal, this book will help you get there. If your goal is to understand similarities between various martial arts, this book will help you get there. If your goal is to understand and improve your technique, this book will help you get there. As you "get there," it may also help you simplify the process and bring some unity to your understanding of how and why martial arts techniques work as they do.

# INTRODUCTION

Today is your first day on the *tatami*. You're lined up around the edge of the mat in traditional protocol. The *dojo* is quiet except for the sound of the small waterfall in the background. *Sensei* enters and bows onto the mat.

The senior student calls the class to attention and there is a formal bow-in. Once that's completed, everyone sits down as sensei calls out his *uke* to demonstrate tonight's new technique.

As the technique is shown two to three times, it is quiet enough to hear a pin drop. Sensei finishes his demonstration, bows off to his uke and commands the class to work on the new technique.

You watched carefully—or you thought you did. You listened to what sensei had to say—but he didn't say anything. You tried to process how the technique worked—but have no idea what really happened.

In fact, you realize that you have no idea what to do or how to do it.

So you muddle through until you figure it out or another student or sensei helps you along the path of understanding.

You begin to realize that there has to be something behind the calm movements of your sensei that you're missing. Is your sensei in command of some special "force" or "energy" of which you have no understanding? How does he seem to capture and use his opponent's energy so effectively—and with very little of his own effort, apparently? What little "trick" did he use to make the technique work? How does he make it look so simple?

The most important question now comes to the forefront: Can I learn this stuff? If your answer is "yes," the next question is: How long will I have to study to become as good as my sensei? The last question, which you probably won't ask, is: Why or how does this stuff work?

It is this last question that serves as the basis for this book. It's possible for you to study an art for years and not understand how physics and anatomy affect body movement. It's also possible to study an art for many years and not realize the similarity of many techniques, even if done to different extremities in different directions. It is also possible to not see commonalities in techniques between different *ryu* (styles) of one art or even different martial arts.

By the time you finish this book, you will know how and why techniques work, as well as basic concepts that can simplify the learning process and help you master your art more effectively. By understanding the kinesthetic movements of techniques and the physics involved, it is possible to simplify your art while at the same time multiplying your technical knowledge. This process was described to a limited scale in my first two books, *Jujitsu: Basic Techniques of the Gentle Art* and *Jujitsu: Intermediate Techniques of the Gentle Art*.

The inspiration for this book, however, comes from Professor Steve Heremia, who resides in New Zealand. I had the opportunity to meet him at Camp Danzan Ryu in 1987. We have corresponded ever since. Professor Heremia is a tremendously giving and respected sensei in the martial arts community. He has reduced *jujitsu* down to 10—that's right, just 10—basic or core movements. Everything in the ryu he teaches comes from those 10 movements.

By the time you finish this book, you should be on your way to having a better understanding of your art and how it works. Such knowledge is critical if you plan to become a well-respected sensei. After all, your students will ask questions and they deserve a competent answer beyond: "Work hard and you'll eventually 'get it,'" or "Be patient and let experience be your teacher."

I'm not talking about this book giving you immediate gratification or providing you with long-kept secrets of the masters that will make your martial arts life easier. If you are going to master your art, you must simplify it as Professor Heremia has done. The basic core movements must be absolutely second nature to you. With that understanding, you will realize how simple your art is—much to everyone else's amazement and frustration.

This book also has a second purpose: to help you establish better control of yourself through self-relaxation and meditation. As a successful martial artist, it is absolutely essential that you have control over your emotions and the many daily stresses that affect your composure. Every generation lives in a stressful world. There are external and internal stresses that affect us all. It is how we deal with those stresses that help or hinder our internal calm or *ki*. Therefore, part of your sensei training is to have a means of maintaining your ki.

Self-relaxation and meditation techniques can be simple yet effective. Realistically, meditation and self-relaxation techniques must be simple because simplicity is the key to success in this area. The ability to master this part of your training will not only make you a better sensei, but a better person, spouse, parent or participant in any other type of positive relationship.

Thus the goal of this book is twofold. One purpose is to help you develop an understanding of your art: how and why techniques work as you simplify your art. The second purpose is to help you develop an understanding yourself and how you can best meet your own needs and the needs of others. This is a tall order. However, if you are truly going to become a well-respected and knowledgeable teacher, these are the two basic skills that you must master.

As a true sensei, you will be a model, participant, leader and guide for the students in your dojo and in the larger martial arts community. By mastering your art, you will become knowledgeable and self-confident yet humble and open-minded, secure and willing to help others. With this position also come increased responsibility and the need for humility. For it is in being humble that you will gain respect from your students and the martial arts community.

The first verse of the following poem appeared in the preface of *Jujitsu: Intermediate Techniques of the Gentle Art* and in *Jujitsu Nerve Techniques: The Invisible Weapon of Self-Defense*. This poem can now be presented in its two-verse version:

**Two Inseparable Friends**

Control is the key.
Patience is the key.
The key is not trying at all.
Self-control is the key.
Ki is the key to success.

Control is the ki.
Patience is the ki.
The ki is not trying at all.
Self-control is the ki.
Ki is the ki to success.

Simplicity is the key.
Humbleness is the key.
Inner calm is the key.
Mushin is the key.
Ki is the key to success.

Simplicity is the ki.
Humbleness is the ki.
Inner calm is the ki.
Mushin is the ki.
Ki is the ki to success.

# CONTENTS

# PART I: PHYSICS AND THE MARTIAL ARTS

Did you study algebra and physics in school? Do you know what kinesthetics is? How about an xyz graph? What about quadrants, spheres, planes and bases? What's a lever, fulcrum, effort and load? Is this a math book? A science book?

Actually, it's both. If you plan to have a thorough understanding of your martial art, you need to get beyond the simple memorization of *kata* and techniques. I'm not diminishing the value of them; learning kata and techniques can be tremendously valuable and will help you *know* your art. However, quantity is not the same as quality.

There are between 20 and 40 basic kata in most styles of *jujitsu*, and the same can probably be said of most martial arts. To be even more specific, there are more than 800 specific techniques and variations in the art of *budoshin* jujitsu. Knowing these will indicate a high level of technical knowledge and competence, and no one will question your skill level. That's what promotions and belts are for—to indicate technical proficiency. However, holding a particular rank, grade or belt does not necessarily indicate an understanding of your art.

There is a difference between knowing something and understanding how and why it does what it does. Knowing how to do something means that you can do it well. Understanding something means that you can rationally and competently explain how and why you're doing it, in an organized manner that others can understand. Why do certain moves need to be made in a particular order? Why is body position and footwork so important? Why is balance critical? Is it better to execute techniques faster? These are among a myriad of questions students can ask about their art. Some *sensei* are inclined to answer their students' questions, some are not.

My sensei, Jack Seki, rarely explained things because he thought it was not his responsibility to teach the finer points of jujitsu. He told us that it was far more important to watch what his body did rather than listen to what he said. He would physically move our bodies or extremities into the correct positions, and that was as far as he went. He believed that if you, the student, could figure out the finer points by yourself through observation and practice, it would make a more lasting impression that way. His approach was valid and rational.

As a public-school teacher, I know that if a student figures out something on his own, his chances of retaining that information over a long period of time increase tremendously. However, I can't in good conscience allow my students to ponder every major idea I present to them until they have a revelation regarding its logic or validity. As a sensei, I see part of my role as helping students get over learning hurdles. Sometimes, a simple hint or helpful hand will have a major impact on their learning process, particularly if their learning curve has stagnated or plateaued.

Like my sensei, I often move my students' bodies and extremities so they're in the correct position to execute techniques correctly. I explain why they are doing what they are doing so they see the logical sequence and rationale of their movements. If they understand this relationship, they can concentrate on other aspects of their training, which includes gaining some technical insight on their own.

As a student, it took me more than a year to figure out exactly how to correctly set a figure-4 armbar 100 percent of the time. I was totally inept at executing *hane goshi* (an inner sweeping hip throw) until after I became a second-degree black belt. The ability to suddenly execute these two techniques well was sort of a revelation to me. Upon such revelations, sensei Seki would say, "Ah, Geogie, you finally got it." (Seki had difficulty pronouncing "r" sounds.) With those few words, I knew I had figured out something that would be a major turning point in my training. I had acquired knowledge. In some cases, it would take me a few years to understand why certain techniques worked. Understanding this required more than merely accepting that certain parts of my body had to be in certain positions.

It was only in the past few years that I realized that traditional martial arts concepts, such as *saiki tanden, ki,* balance and *kuzushi,* could be explained by using basic math and science concepts. Working to understand this relationship has helped me understand how and why techniques work and how most techniques are based on a relatively few common movements of the human body. Kinesthetics, the study of body movement under certain or specific conditions, helped me move from having technical knowledge of my art to also understanding how other arts functioned.

Like I said, one of the purposes of this book is to help you develop an understanding of your art: why it works like it does. This book is about my martial art, jujitsu, and your martial art, whatever that might be. When sensei Seki promoted me to black belt so the late Bill Fromm and I could teach at a local YMCA, he said, "Bill knows more techniques, and you're a teacher. You will figure it out as you teach." So this part of the book is carrying out my sensei's request to "figure it out." Because jujitsu is the parent art of judo, *aikido* and many forms of karate, I hope that, by understanding the elements that make jujitsu work, you will develop a greater understanding of why your martial art works, whether it is a *do* (way) or *jitsu* (art). It is this understanding that will result in tremendous growth—exponential at times—in your technical knowledge and proficiency and that will help you master your art as a whole. This is what makes a martial art an *art*. This is what makes striving for perfection a lifelong process. You cannot truly understand your martial art, however, unless you know the basics.

## The XYZ-Axis

Stand up straight, with your feet together and your hands at your sides, looking straight ahead. You are now the y-axis of a sphere. Look at or visualize your navel, and move your visualization down about two inches to the center of your torso. This is your center of gravity, also called the saiki tanden, *hara* or (if you're thinking geometry) the origin of the xyz-axis, also known as "0,0,0" or zero point. The y-axis is a straight line, perpendicular to the ground, that extends up between your feet, through your saiki tanden and up through the center of your head.

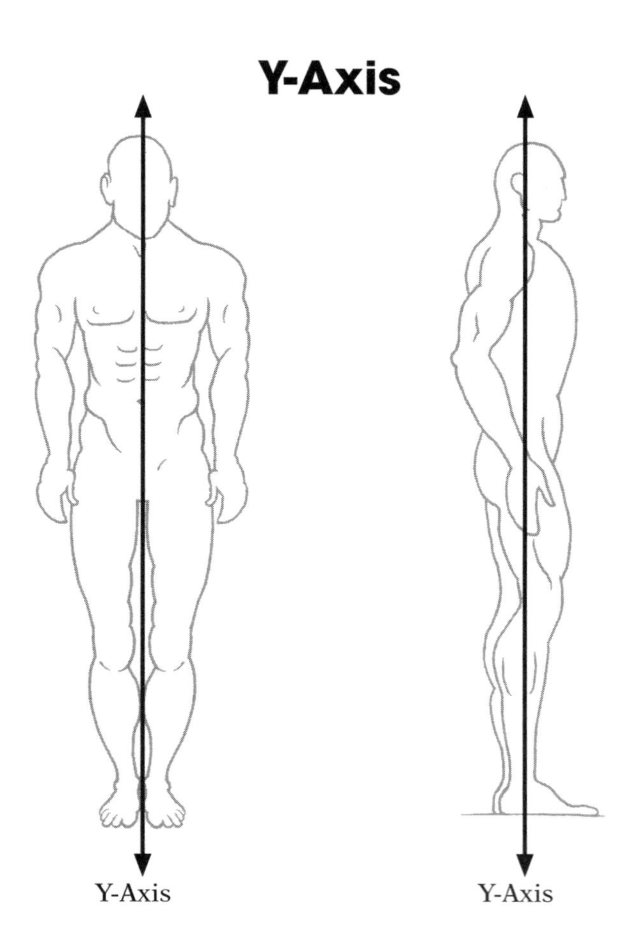

Now look to your left and right. The x-axis extends to your left and right from your center/zero point. If you rotate your hips, torso or shoulder to the left or right, you are moving the x-axis.

Last, look in front of you and (as best you can) behind you. This is the z-axis. The z-axis goes through your saiki tanden, perpendicular to the x- and y-axis.

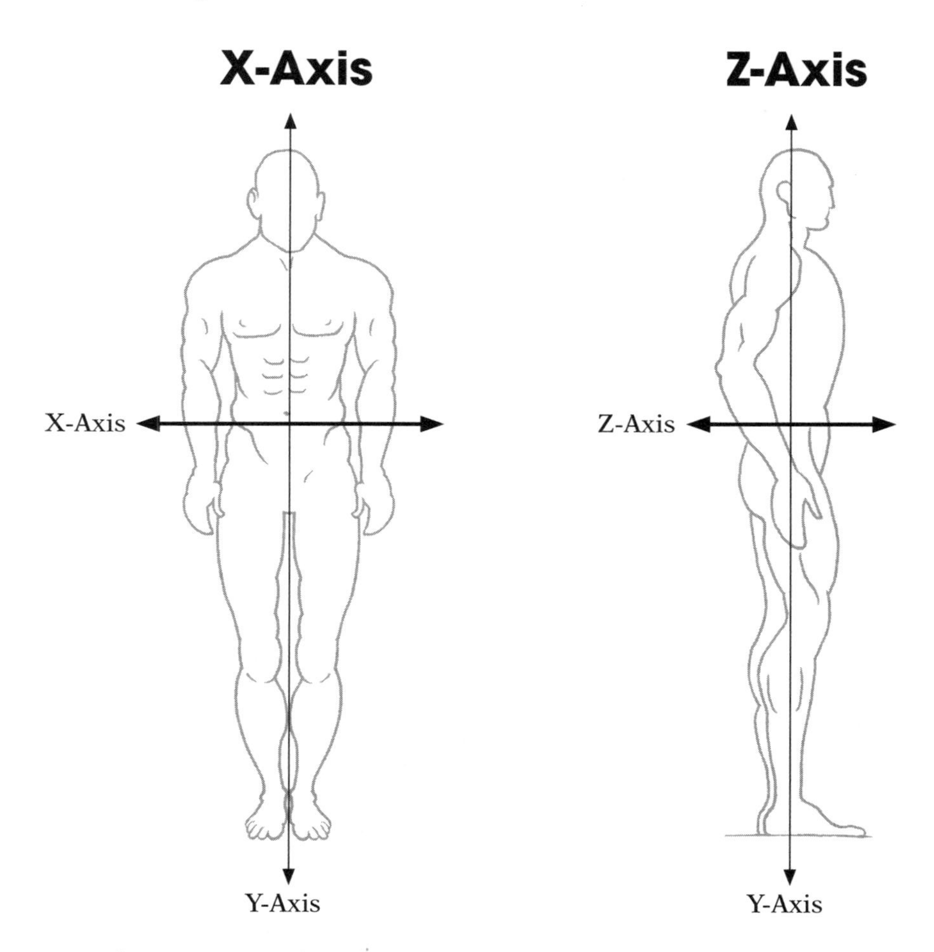


If you can visualize these three axes going through your saiki tanden, you have probably mastered the most difficult concept in this book, and this visualization is absolutely essential in understanding the concepts that follow. Knowing where the three axes cross will give you an awareness of where ki originates and how your head, shoulders, arms, hands, torso, legs and feet must be aligned for the most effective execution of techniques.

## XYZ-Axis

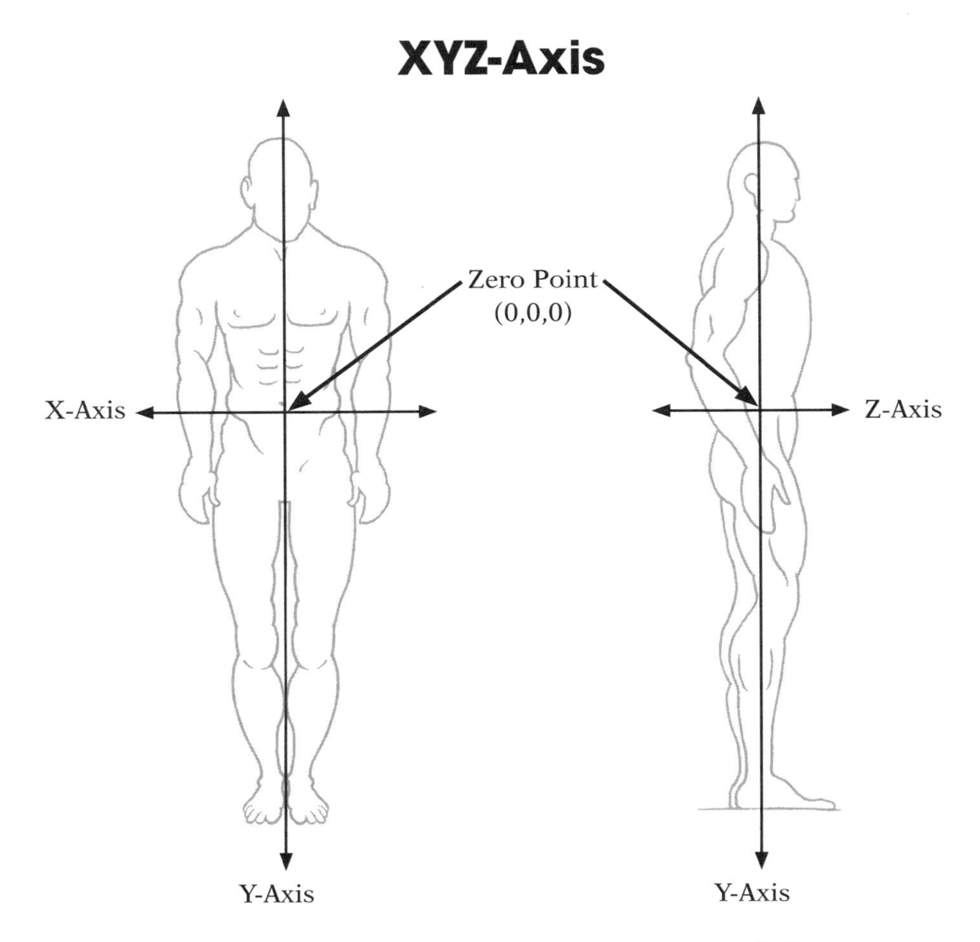


The saiki tanden, or zero point, is also the source of all movement. You must maintain your center of balance as you execute any technique if you want it to work properly. This means that you will have to move your body and, in doing so, you will also move the xyz-axis. The xyz-axis is not rigid or fixed in one place; it moves as you move. If your body goes up or down, the zero point will go up or down the y-axis. As you turn to your left or right, the x- and z-axis will rotate on the y-axis. Even if you are sitting or lying on the ground, the xyz-axis rule will function, although your negative "z" range will be greatly reduced or totally eliminated, and your x-axis will be restricted. (See diagram on next page.)

# Restricted X-Axis

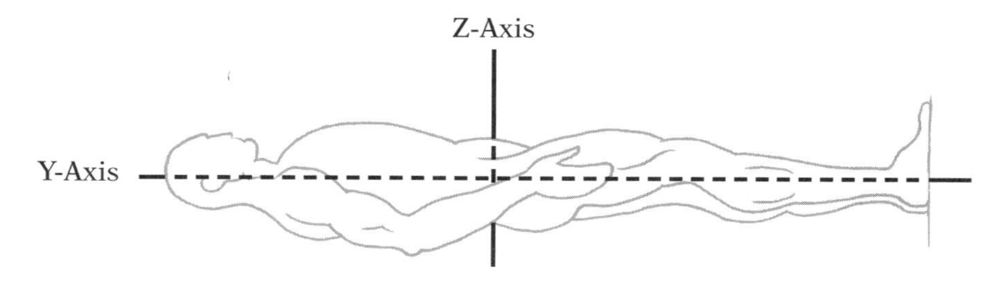


There's one more factor that must be considered in maintaining your balance: footwork. If your sensei is anything like mine, the most common instructional Japanese word he used in class was kuzushi (the ability to maintain your balance or maintain your balance while unbalancing your opponent). If pressed to use English, he used the words "balance" and "footwork."

*Balance, balance, balance! Kuzushi, kuzushi, kuzushi!* This concept applies to every aspect of your life, be it an interpersonal relationship, winning a contract in a competitive economic environment, winning a battle (and hopefully the war) during a military conflict, executing a technique perfectly in the *dojo*, and surviving a street confrontation. In short, your life must be balanced if you are going to live long and happily.

Balance is the ability to maintain your base or foundation. In an ideal situation, it means you have to keep your y-axis perpendicular to the ground (in karate and aikido) or parallel to the y-axis of your opponent (in judo). Balance is maintained by moving your feet and/or raising or lowering your center point in order to keep your y-axis properly aligned with your opponent's or in relation to the surface you're on.

The correct placement and movement of your feet is absolutely essential to the proper use of you and your opponent's ki. The placement of your feet and pelvis forms the support from which your ki can be most efficiently and effectively generated and used. Proper footwork also allows your body to turn on the y-axis so that your hands, arms, legs and feet can function effectively relative to the x- and z-axis.

There is one aspect of footwork that most martial artists agree on: A person has better balance if both feet are on the ground. If you lift one foot, your balance has to shift to the other foot, which is not as secure. Judo, aikido and jujitsu practitioners know that the most effective time to take an opponent off-balance is when he lifts a foot off the ground or, even better, the moment before he places his foot back on the ground. This is why soft-art practitioners slide their feet rather than step. They rarely allow their feet to leave the ground, because that would expose them to having a foot swept or being otherwise unbalanced. Sliding your feet also makes it easier to re-establish a firm base or easily shift your balance if someone attempts to pull or push you off-balance.

Let's return to the xyz-axis that you've visualized. Mathematically, each of the axes can go on into infinity. If you become engaged in a conversation about ki, you will soon realize that the same concept applies and that ki can be extended beyond your physical body to an unknown distance. There are exercises you can learn that will improve your sixth sense (we'll cover this later), making you more sensitive to other people's ki or energy flow. Realistically, though, your own xyz-axis is limited by how far you can reach in every direction with your hands and feet from the y-axis

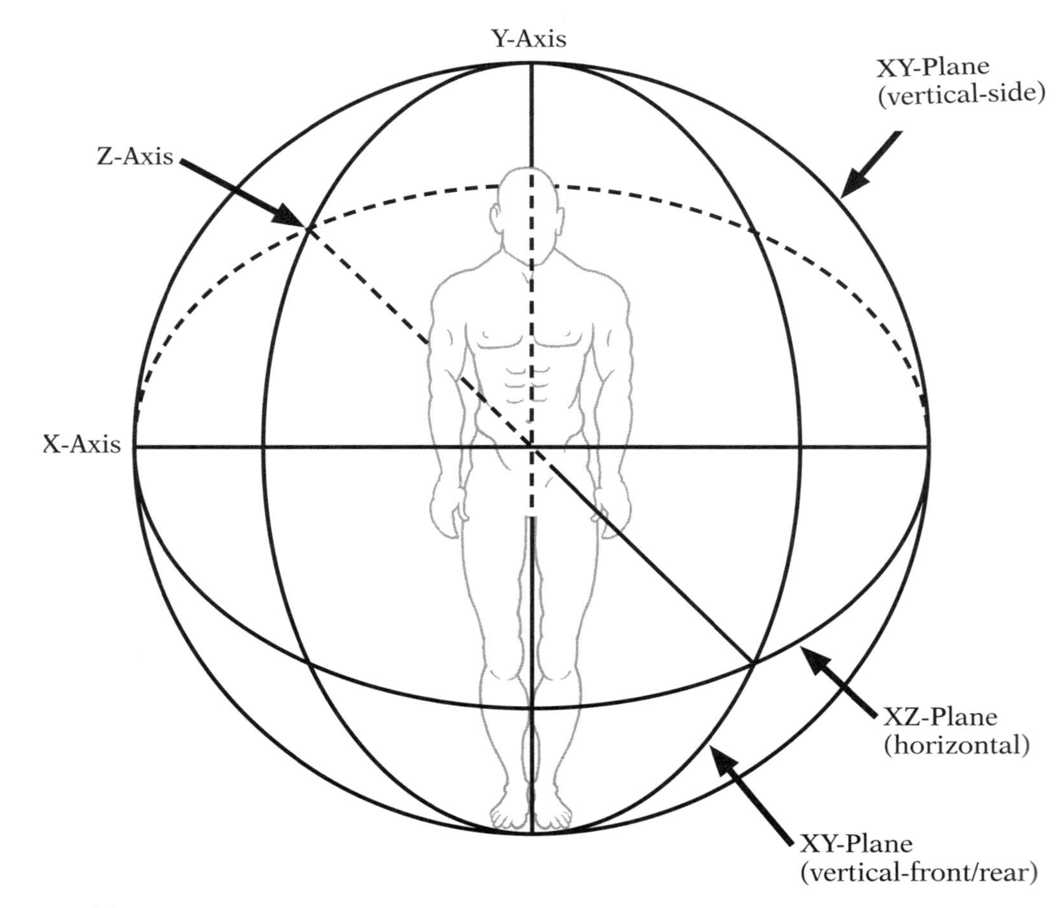

while remaining balanced. If you try this, you will find that you create an imaginary sphere, with your saiki tanden as the center.

The sphere you create is the area within which you can make contact with your opponent. When you and your opponent's spheres interact, the relative positions of your y-axes will determine what offensive or defensive action you can take. It's sort of like a Venn diagram, which is used to illustrate commonalities and differences between two items, ideas, etc.

The overlapping spheres indicate where the opponents can make physical contact.

This may sound cumbersome, but there is a method to the madness. What you can do to attack or defend yourself is always dependent on you and your opponent's position. By reducing both of your positions to two spheres, rather than two xyz-axes of indefinite range, it becomes easier to visualize what techniques will work. So let's now look more specifically at different types of actions and responses along the xyz-axis within your sphere.

As stated previously, the effectiveness of a technique is based on your sphere in relation to your opponent's sphere. As you visualize your sphere and your attacker's, keeping the xyz-axis in mind, you'll recognize that there are eight quadrants or zones. How you use each of these zones depends on your art and your opponent's actions. Every technique you use will be within these eight quadrants, and if executed properly, all of your techniques will be executed with the axis lines fixed relative to your saiki tanden. The movement of your body or extremities from the initial position will be either in a straight line or a circle, depending on the situation and your technical knowledge.

## Straight Technique

Assume the ready position.

As the attacker swings, block the punch at a 90-degree angle.

Raise your right hand.

Execute a straight palm strike to the attacker's nose.

## Circular Technique

Assume the ready position.

As the attacker swings, step to the left and deflect it with your left forearm.

Push his right arm down.

Continue the downward motion with your left arm and grab his right shoulder with your right hand.

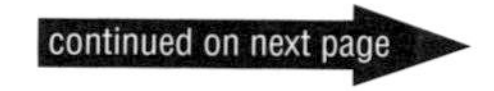
continued on next page

Continue the clockwise motion, pulling the attacker forward.

Pivot back with your right foot and kneel on your left knee, bringing the attacker to the floor, and finish with a shoulder lock.

## Hard and Soft Responses: Blocks, Strikes and Techniques

If your movement is in a straight line or at a right angle to your opponent, it could be considered a "hard" response, which is to say that your blocks will be at a right angle to the direction of the attack and make hard contact with the opponent's extremity.

Right-angle (90-degree) blocks are generally considered to be "hard" blocks used to stop the forward momentum of an attack.

Note that the block is done with the forearm, not with the wrist or hand. The hand is open to allow the defender to quickly trap the forearm, if necessary.

Hard blocks of this type can stop or redirect the attack in another direction. Hard blocks can, if directed toward a nerve center on the extremity, temporarily stun or incapacitate that extremity. In some cases, a solidly delivered block can even fracture the attacking extremity. Regardless of the physical outcome, the ultimate purpose of a hard block is to distract or off-balance the attacker and make him vulnerable to a response. In this sense, "off-balance" means physically moving your opponent in a direction he didn't plan to go by taking advantage of and accentuating his movement, or by creating a psychological distraction, either of which will create a 0.3- to 0.7-second reaction gap that can be used to "get ahead" of your opponent's movements.

A hard response occurs when the defender counters at a 90- or 180-degree angle to the attack.

Use a right-angle block to deflect the blow.

Deliver a palm strike to the sternum, destroying the attacker's balance and opening him up to a follow-through technique. It is often easier and more effective to palm strike with your fingers pointed slightly outward.

Hard-response striking techniques have certain characteristics. After blocking your opponent's attack, you should immediately take advantage of the opening (or "off-balancing") you have created. If you're responding with a strike or kick to the front of the attacker, it will usually be in line with your z-axis, and your body will rotate on the x-axis to the appropriate angle. Keep in mind that strikes and kicks do not originate from the hand or foot. If properly executed, they emanate from the saiki tanden, and your body will rotate and position itself to give your extremities the most power and the most concentrated ki.

Effective kicks are more difficult to deliver. Although they can provide a much bigger impact than a strike, kicks require a greater shift in your balance and require a more critical maintenance of your center of balance. If properly executed, a kick will develop greater momentum and

When delivering a strike, it is always important to create maximum momentum.

Note how the x-axis changes and the hips rotate forward.

move more mass. Kicks, particularly ones that extend above the saiki tanden, result in a floating base and a very powerful delivery if executed properly and can result in bruises, abrasions and, in some cases, fractures and serious internal injuries to the opponent. To use kicks as part of your self-defense repertoire, you must realize that your base is not as secure, and if not delivered quickly, your leg can be blocked and trapped by your opponent, leaving you wide-open for a counter-technique. High kicks, especially those that require both feet being off the ground, can result in a serious commitment of ki over a relatively long period of time, which can be a disadvantage in a street situation.

An alternative to the hard response is the soft (or circular) response. A soft-response block is always an acute-angle (less than 90-degree) block. It could be argued that the angle of a soft block is acute because the direction of a soft block usually originates from the same direction as the attack itself.

The more acute the angle (between the direction of the attacking extremity—as the base line—and the direction of the block from the blocking extremity), the softer the block. In fact, if the defender is moving his xy-axis in line with the xy-axis of his attacker, the attacker may not notice the block at all because the block would actually be a trap, seizing the attacker's ki and using it against him.

As the attacker strikes, deflect the blow outward with a 45-degree block with your left hand while stepping in with your right foot. The right hand is ready to block another strike, if necessary.

Grab the top of his right sleeve at the wrist with your left hand, and grab the same sleeve below the shoulder with your right hand. Lift his arm up and away from you in a rowing motion and step back with your left foot, turning your body.

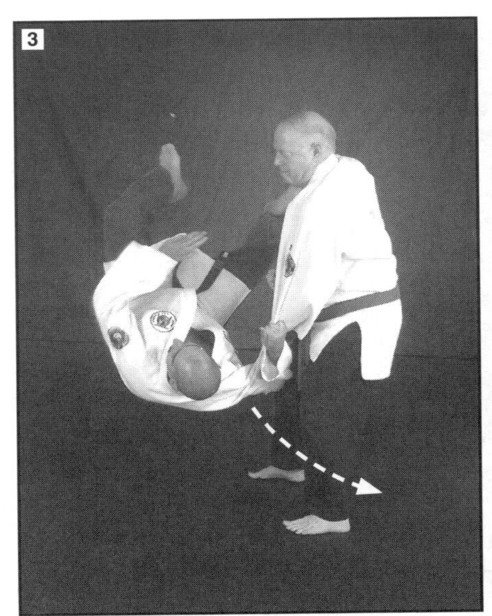


Continue the circular motion and throw your opponent.

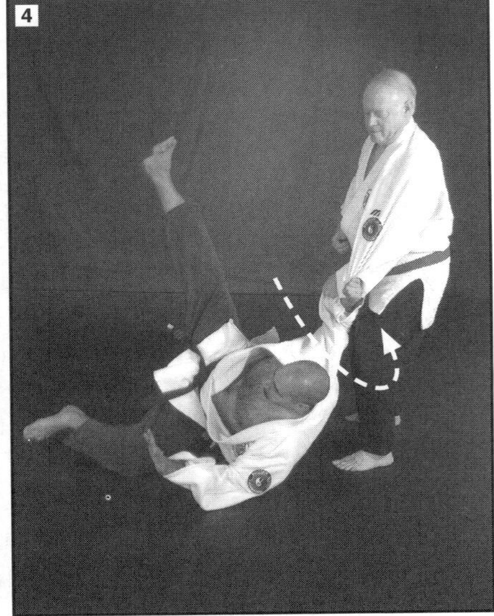


Release your opponent's sleeve with your right hand as he falls.

As with a hard block, a soft block's intention is to distract, off-balance and open the attacker up to a counter-response. A soft block will usually deflect an attack rather than stop it, and it creates the advantage of two options for the defender:

**1.** Once he deflects the attack and changes its direction, he can move in a straight line to stop and counter the attacker's ki, or

**2.** He can move in a circular direction and redirect the attacker's ki, melding it with his own.

The latter occurs when the defender aligns his y-axis with the y-axis of his opponent, becoming, in effect, the center of the circle. Once this is done, he can throw the attacker simply by continuing the circular motion of the attacking extremity and taking a step forward or backward while maintaining his balance. If executed well, the attacker won't even sense

Assume the ready position.

As the attacker strikes, deflect the blow upward and to the left with your left forearm.

continued on next page

Grab his lower sleeve with your left hand, and grab his upper sleeve slightly below his shoulder with your right hand.

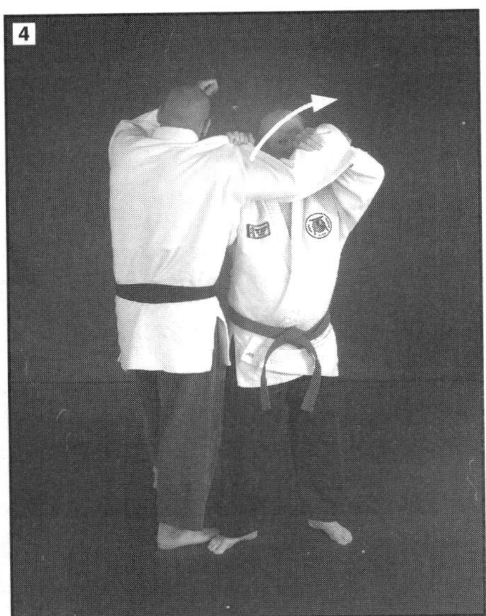


Raise his arm slightly to off-balance him.

Step forward with your left foot and move his arm away and down to execute the throw.

that his ki is being redirected until it's too late to do anything about it.

Circular responses are most commonly found in the "softer" martial arts of jujitsu, judo, aikido and *hapkido*. These "softer" techniques (a real misnomer) include but are not limited to simple releases, control holds, throws, joint locks, pressure-point and nerve attacks, leverage techniques, mat pins and submission techniques.

As a side note, control holds use pain compliance through joint locks and/or pressure points to secure the physical cooperation of the assailant. The effective use of control holds can allow the defender to move an assailant in a desired direction. An extremely effective (and low visibility) control hold is the wrist-twist little-finger brace come along. Although shown here against a cross-wrist grab, it can be used against almost any type of attack.

The attacker grabs your right wrist with his right hand.

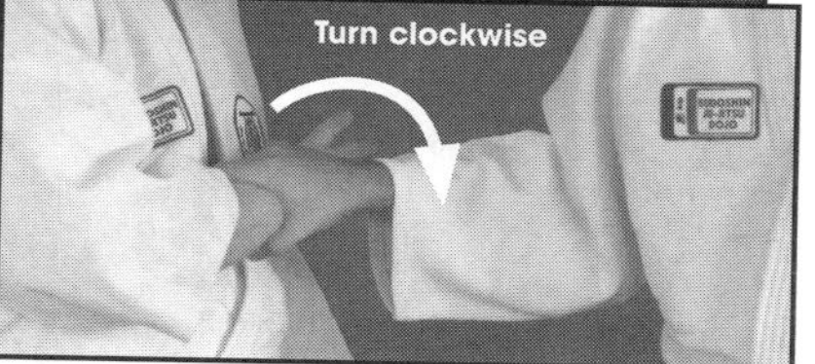


Begin turning your hand clockwise, keeping it close to your body. Be sure to keep your hand open and relaxed.

continued on next page

Continue turning your hand clockwise so it ends up on the outside of his forearm.

Bring your left hand up from underneath.

Grab his little finger with your left hand and brace your thumb on the back of his hand. Continue moving your right hand in a clockwise circle as the attacker loses his grip on your wrist.

Continue rotating his hand clockwise by pulling his little finger across the back of his hand. Notice that his elbow is raised and bent, posing a possible threat.

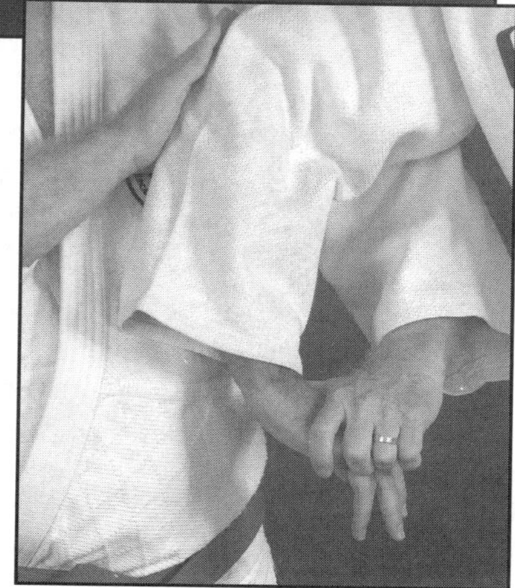

Lower his arm by pulling his little finger farther across the back of his hand, causing more pain. Your right hand can rest on his elbow as a protective barrier in case he tries to counter.

A control hold can even allow the defender to use the assailant as a physical shield against other attackers. Pain-compliance techniques are also very effective in creating the illusion of injury, and seeing their friend in pain can serve as a psychological deterrent to attacks by the assailant's cohorts.

Pain-compliance techniques work very well, as long as you don't injure your assailant and cause a fracture, dislocation or sprain. If any of these injuries occur, whether through the use of a control hold or a submission technique, you will no longer be able to control your assailant or use him

When faced with multiple attackers, you can use one opponent as a shield against the others. The key is to use an effective control hold that uses pain to secure the attacker's cooperation.

as a shield because his sole goal will be to get away from you. The severe pain will cause his adrenaline level to skyrocket, giving him additional strength. You cannot control a person in this situation; the pain created by the injury (plus the aggravation to the injury if the hold is maintained) will be far greater than what you could create with the hold alone.

Circular responses can also be manifested in other soft responses, such as throws. Throws range from the simple *mae yubi nage* (forward finger throw) as seen in aikido and jujitsu to devastating body throws, such as the *karada makikomi* (body winding throw) and the variety of *ushiro nage* (rear throws) found in judo, jujitsu and hapkido.

## Mae Yubi Nage (Forward Finger Throw)

*Mae yubi nage* is simple but effective. As the attacker reaches toward you, block his hand with your right forearm and step to your left.

Slide your hand down and grab his wrist.

Continue the downward motion, turning his hand slightly so his palm is facing you.

Reach up with your left hand and grab at least three of his fingers.

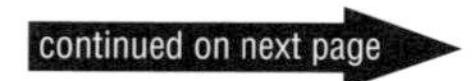
continued on next page

Apply pressure to the base of his knuckles and bend his fingers back. This will force the attacker to raise his arm.

To execute the throw, push forward against the back of his hand as you step forward with your right foot.

When the attacker lands, keep holding his fingers for a possible follow-up submission.

## Karada Makikomi (Body Winding Throw)

The *karada makikomi* is another throw that demonstrates circular movement. As the attacker punches, block outward while stepping in with your left foot.

Trap and hook the attacker's right wrist and turn into the attacker, stepping forward with your right foot and blocking his right ankle. Raise your right arm.

Bring your right arm around his head. Note that, as you continue to turn to your left and lean forward slightly, his head and body will align itself with the y-axis of your body.

Continue to lean forward and turn to your left, kneeling on your right knee.

continued on next page

The momentum from his weight will cause the attacker to land underneath you, in position for a variety of pins or submission holds. (Your *uke* should use a strong *kiai* to get the air out of his lungs; this will help reduce the impact of the throw.)

Raise the attacker's right arm slightly and slip your right upper thigh under his upper arm.

Bring your right leg over the arm and lock your ankle in the crook of your left knee, finishing with a figure-4 armbar.

Throwing an opponent gently can intimidate without really causing injury, but slamming him on the ground can cause severe, multiple injuries. Fractures, dislocations and a concussion can result from a single throw executed with the effective use of ki. Throwing an opponent against a solid object—like a curb, newsstand or car—can create additional impact injuries, and throwing him at or on his cohorts can create a barrier to other attacks.

A story that validates how soft techniques can cause serious injuries involves a young lady with a midlevel rank in jujitsu. She was walking to her car in a parking structure when a man attacked her from behind and got her in a bear hug. She immediately dropped her weight and executed a *tai-otoshi* (drop throw). Her assailant went over her right side, hitting the concrete. The young lady immediately stepped back into *tachi waza* (the ready position), anticipating that her attacker would get up and resume the assault. He didn't. He had sustained a concussion, dislocated shoulder and broken ribs from hitting the ground. She was astounded at the damage she had caused—all from a simple throw.

The ability of the martial artist to throw an assailant with control requires three elements. First, the defender must have the skill to manipulate his and his attacker's ki while executing the throw. When I was a junior high-school teacher in the early 1970s, one of my ninth-grade homeroom students, about my size, who had a generally tough reputation, had heard that I knew jujitsu and wanted to find out if what he heard was true. So one day during lunch, he came up behind me and put an object across the front of my neck. Automatically reacting to the attack, I immediately struck his upper arm to get the object away and swept him with a *harai goshi* (an outside sweeping throw). It was only when I saw him going over that I realized he was a student—my student. I pulled up on his arm and he landed relatively gently and with no injuries, the pen still in his hand. Needless to say, he had a worthwhile learning experience. I also never had any problems with him or his friends after that point.

Second, the defender must have an awareness of his environment—where he is and what is around him. Again, this can be called the martial artist's "sixth sense." If you know what's around you, it can be used by you. Many years ago, as I approached the left door of my van to get something for a picnic my wife and I were having, two men approached me. One came toward me from my left side and one from the front of the van. The one to my left asked if I had five dollars. By the time he had finished his question, I had the minivan door opened between him and me. I looked directly at him and simply said, "No." He and his friend backed away, turned and left.

Although a physical confrontation didn't ensue, part of my success (if you can call it that) was owing to my awareness of my environment: I used the minivan door as a barrier/shield. Also, because of my training/sixth sense, I realized that the question, "Do you have five dollars?" was a distraction to get me to reach for money or get my wallet out. It's very similar to being stopped on the street and asked, "Do you know what time it is?" The verbal distraction didn't work, plus they found their path blocked by the van door.

Third, the defender must be sure to align his y-axis parallel with his attacker's y-axis, with his saiki tanden just below his attacker's saiki tanden.

Parallel body alignment is critical to the success of many throws.

The attacker (left) reaches, creating forward momentum.

Deflect his right arm and step in with your right foot.

Continue turning to the left, pulling the attacker toward you and setting him up for a one-arm hip throw (*ippon seoi nage*). Note that your y-axes should be parallel and his body should be tight against yours.

Squat down, bringing your x-axis($x_1$) below his x-axis ($x_2$).

Straighten your legs with the attacker resting on your back, his *saiki tanden* slightly above yours.

Continue turning to the left to execute the throw.

When the attacker lands, he is in perfect position for a figure-4 armbar.

After a throw or takedown, circular responses may also result in a pin, joint-lock submission or hard response—a strike or kick to a vital area, for example. All of these are viable choices, assuming your opponent hasn't been injured by the impact of the takedown. If you use any type of ground-submission technique, the ultimate outcome may be a choke out (unconsciousness), joint dislocation or fracture. On the ground, the relation of your xyz-axis to his is more critical to the success of your technique than when you're standing. While executing a choke or upper-extremity lock, your center of balance should be close to his upper quadrants and as parallel to his x-axis as possible, whether you are perpendicular or parallel to your opponent.

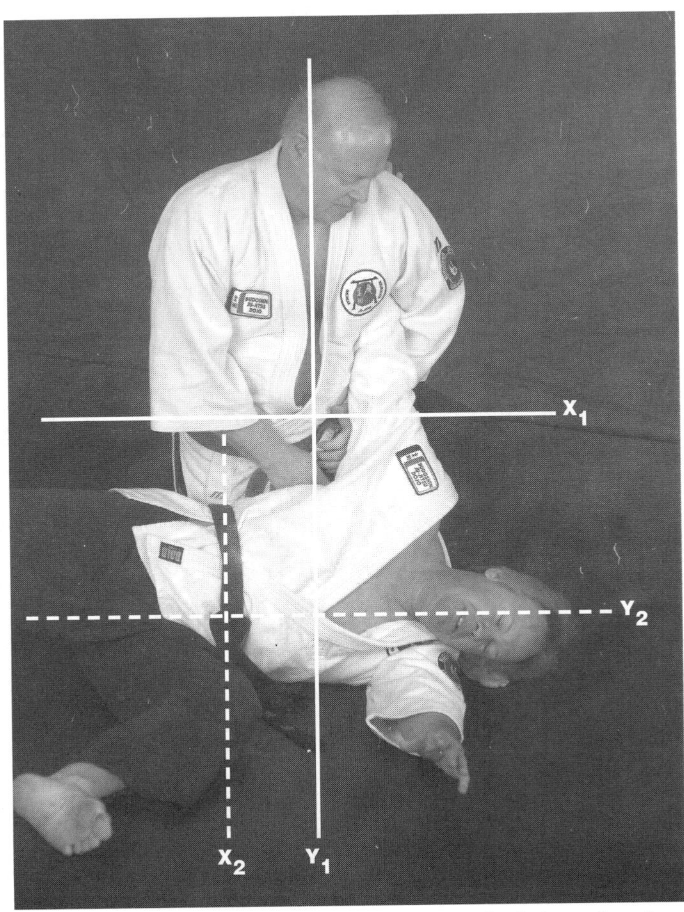


Axis alignment is far more critical on the ground, where the fast execution of submission holds is an essential part of effective self-defense.

If you are on your opponent's back, you will be more effective in keeping him down if you keep his hips on the ground. The key to being successful is to have your saiki tanden just below his, thereby placing most of your body weight just below his hips. Whatever you do from that point is dependent on your control of his hips—his x-axis. It is also important that you turn the insteps of your feet inward, against his upper thighs. This makes it impossible for your opponent to slide his leg up and roll you over.

If your *saiki tanden* is above your opponent's, he will be able to use his legs and lower-body strength to gain leverage.

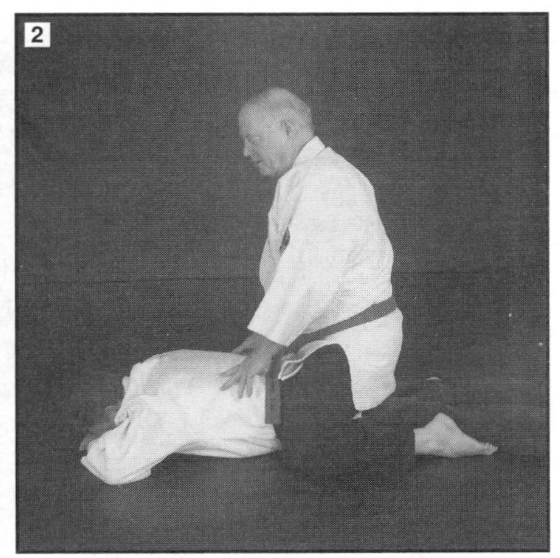


Instead, sit below his saiki tanden to control his hips.

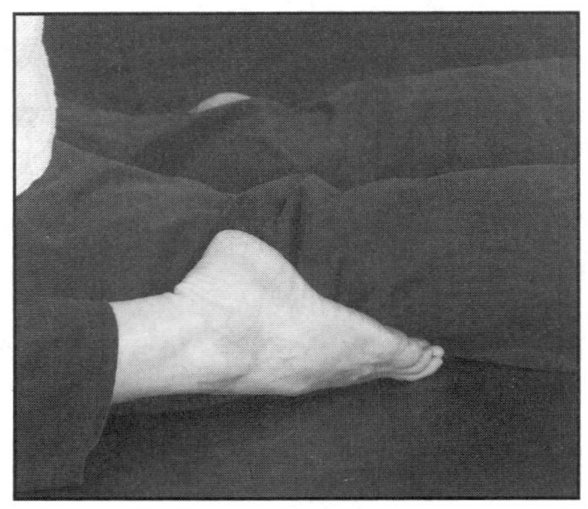

Remember to always turn your toes inward against the attacker's thighs.

There is one more concept to deal with regarding soft and hard responses. As with many aspects of the martial arts, it can be said that opposites attract (*yin* and *yang*). Therefore, as a general rule, straight attacks should be met with circular/soft responses. Conversely, circular attacks should be met with straight/hard responses. In reality, this rule can be applied to your initial response to the attack or to your entire series of responses. It is also possible (and sometimes more effective) to switch between soft and hard responses, depending on how your attacker responds to them. Developing this awareness should be part of your martial arts training.

## Commitment and Flexibility

Your training should consist of commitment and the realization that the techniques you use won't always work. These concepts are interrelated.

On the street, there are no second chances. If you realize you did a technique wrong and it's not working, you can't ask the attacker to stop and start over again. So, on one hand, you have to commit to defending yourself and finishing the technique if it's workable. This goes back to training in your dojo. You don't practice hitting a target—you practice hitting *through* the target. Likewise, you don't stop going through the movements of a throw just because your opponent starts to move; you finish the technique. Why? Because you're training your ki to flow in a direction that will cause your opponent's ki to be used against him, thus allowing your technique to succeed. If you have positioned your respective xyz-axes correctly, trained your ki and trained yourself to complete the move, technique, kata, etc., you have commitment. You will be more successful in the execution of techniques because your axes and origin points are aligned in a manner to maximize the use of you and your attacker's ki. Success is inevitable!

Commitment is also essential because you might inadvertently start a technique backward. Rather than turning a wrist to your left, you might turn it to your right. What do you do now? Again, you cannot start over, and it may not be wise to reverse direction to execute the technique you wanted. Instead, you've got to continue with what you've got. As my sensei said to his students (and as I say to mine), "Go! Go! Go! Keep going! Keep going!"

Jujitsu is a very forgiving art. If you start a move backward and keep going, guess what? You will inevitably end up with another technique. If you want to execute a hand throw (*te nage*) but go the wrong way and instead apply a wrist lock (*tekubi shimi waza*), you have to continue with that. If, while trying to do a corkscrew (*ude guruma*), you turn the arm counterclockwise instead of clockwise, you'll end up with a shoulder-lock rear takedown (*ude guruma ushiro*). And that's OK. Just continue and flow. An awareness of this concept is an essential element in learning the art. On the street, you have to keep moving. It's part of your commitment.

There are times, however, when you commit to a technique and realize that it isn't working the way you want. Maybe your and your opponent's axes aren't lined up. Maybe his ki is resisting yours. Whatever the reason, you still don't get a second chance. What you *do* get, however, is the ability to change what you are doing to make your defense successful. This is called *mushin* ("no mind")—a concept that works only if you have a good technical background and sufficient practice. A good technical background provides you with a variety of techniques that can be used against a particular attack, and sufficient practice allows you to be competent in the execution of those techniques and no conscious effort is required to use them or switch between them. Practice also creates awareness of your and your opponent's xyz-axis, their relationship, and how to modify techniques appropriately to execute a workable defense. (Like the sixth sense, the concept of mushin will be discussed further in this book.)

To summarize the concept and effective use of the xyz-axis, you should be aware of the following:

- If you can visualize the xyz-axis and see each line crossing through your saiki tanden, you've probably mastered the most difficult concept in this book.
- Your saiki tanden—your zero point—is the source of all balanced movements made by your body.
- Proper footwork and foot placement is essential to maintaining your center of balance.
- How you defend yourself is always dependent on your position and your opponent's.
- Hard and soft responses have similar goals but may have different outcomes.
- Opposites attract. A straight attack usually warrants a soft/circular response, and a circular attack usually warrants a hard/straight response.
- There are no second chances on the street. You must have commitment and flexibility to successfully defend yourself.

## Planes

Understanding the xyz-axis and how it functions is critical to your ability to master your art and effectively defend yourself. In looking at the sphere of your effective range, you'll notice that there are three planes: the xy-plane, the xz-plane and the yz-plane.

The xy- and yz-plane can be visualized as vertical, flat discs. The xy-plane rests on your x-axis and encompasses the sideward motion within your sphere. As you pivot to the left or right, the xy-plane follows your x-axis and turns in the same direction.

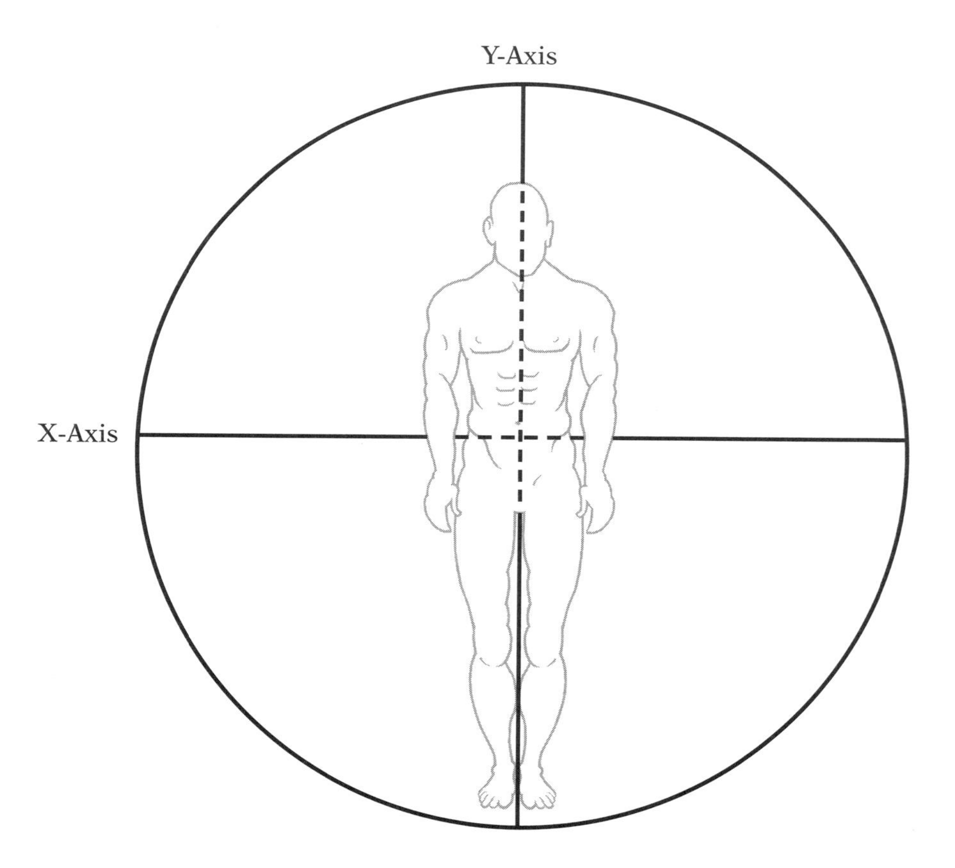

The yz-plane is a vertical plane that rests on the z-axis. It is always perpendicular to the xy-plane and encompasses the forward and backward motion within your sphere. As you pivot, the yz-plane follows your z-axis and turns in the same direction.

## YZ-Plane

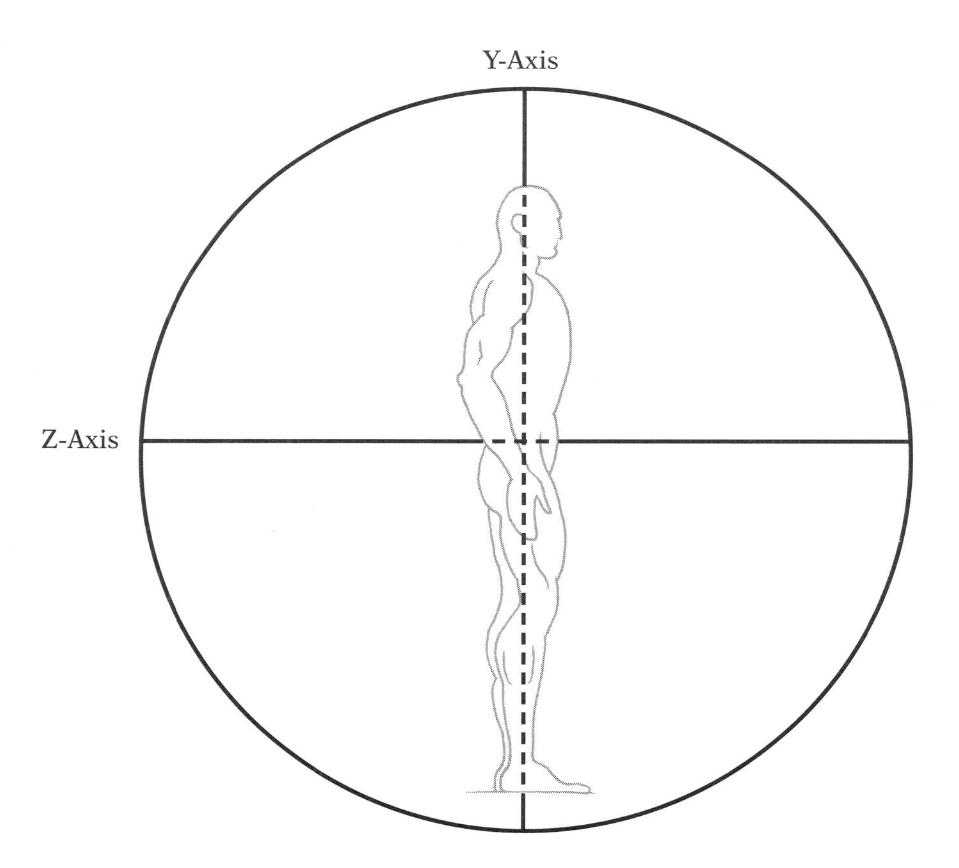


The last plane you need to visualize is the xz-plane. Imagine a disc lying horizontally along the x- and z-axis. This plane serves two roles. First, it indicates where your ki is centered with respect to the ground and within your sphere. This does not mean that your ki can be found anyplace on this plane. The source of your ki is still the saiki tanden, and your techniques ideally should start and end there. However, when visualized with the other two planes, the xz-plane can help guide your execution of techniques in a manner that maximizes the use of your and your attacker's ki to your advantage. The second role of the xz-plane is to create a visualization of your technique's maximum range of effectiveness from the saiki tanden.

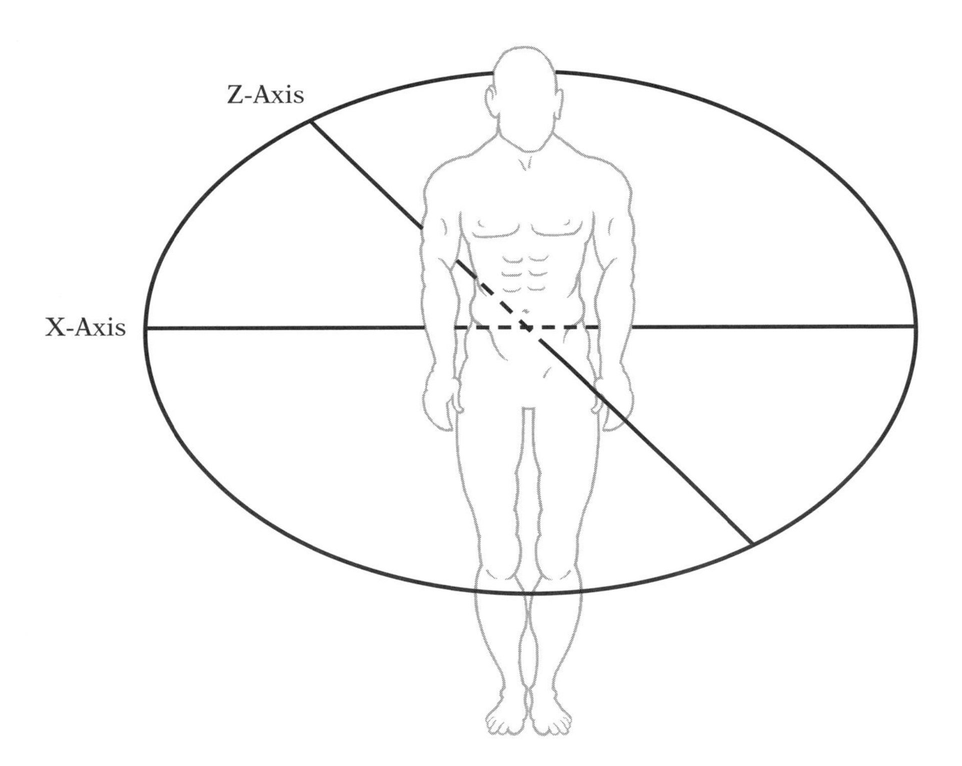


For some people, it's easier to visualize one's place and movement in the sphere by using these three planes rather than the individual lines of the xyz-axis. The use of the three planes makes the eight quadrants of the sphere more definable for some students and helps them visualize the location of their bodies and movements within their spheres. Visualizing all three planes also makes it very clear where your saiki tanden and foot placement must be in order to maintain a balanced sphere, and it can help you realize where the fulcrum of a given technique should be.

## Base

We previously dealt with footwork with respect to your xyz-axis and the importance of proper footwork and foot placement in maintaining your center of balance and establishing a strong foundation for all your techniques, but I should stress that the saiki tanden (either yours or your opponent's) is the base for all techniques.

If you choose to use your saiki tanden as the base for a technique, you must redirect the momentum of your opponent's attack in a direction that will destroy his base. For example, if your attacker strikes at you with a straight/hard attack, you can deflect his blow with a soft/circular deflecting block. If you align your y-axis to make your saiki tanden the center of his ki, you can then use his ki to extend his arm farther than he planned and unbalance him in a forward direction, and then redirect his energy in a circular direction to throw or bring him to the ground.

In executing this technique, you must effectively use your own base, and your footwork must be such that you can rotate into your attacker's field of ki so that your y-axis assumes the center position. This will then allow your x- and z-axis to be properly aligned to absorb and redirect the force of the strike in a circular direction. In short, your goal in counterattacking is to blend your base with the base of your opponent, unbalance him, assume his base and use his energy/ki to execute an effective defensive technique.

Your martial art does not function on the basis of the xyz-axis, planes or bases alone. There is more to your martial art than math. Although these elements set the foundation for the effective execution of techniques unique to your art, they're much like a skeleton, but without the other elements that make the human body move (muscles, ligaments, tendons, etc.), a skeleton is motionless. There is another area we need to look at to help you visualize your art more effectively and master it: kinesthetics, the physics of human body movement.

## Levers and the Fulcrum

Up to this point, we've been doing algebra and geometry. We've been dealing with three-dimensional graphs and spheres, and with your and your opponent's xyz-axis, planes, saiki tanden and their interrelationships. We will continue to look at these elements, but from a completely different perspective. Rather than look at your and your opponent's xyz-axis, we're going to look at the xyz-axis in regard to specific techniques. To examine this relationship properly, we also need to look at the physics of levers and their effect on kinesthetics, and the role of joints, joint locking, rotation and torque. We also need to revisit the concept of balance. You will learn that there are no secrets to properly executed techniques, only well-executed skills that follow simple scientific concepts.

Although the explanations that follow may seem complex at times, they really aren't. All you have to do is follow along step by step. As one of my students recently said to me, "Thank you for using the KISS theory—Keep It Simple, Sensei." The trick to being successful, regardless of your martial art, is to keep it simple. All techniques are made up of a logical series of simple steps or moves. Increasing your familiarity with these small steps will allow you to develop techniques that not only are consistent with the traditions of your martial art but also will appear amazingly complex or advanced at times in spite of their simplicity. If you've gotten this far in this book without getting confused, you're walking. My goal now is to help you learn how to run.

To understand how techniques work, one must understand the concept of levers and how they apply to martial arts techniques. In executing a technique, you generally use part of your body as a fulcrum to completely unbalance your opponent, so you must understand the different types of levers and how they function. Although this may seem like a side trip into a physics classroom, there's no way to skip this information if you really want to understand how your art works.

A lever is a very simple machine used to move a significant amount of weight. All levers use a pivot point, called a fulcrum (F), as the means to use effort (E) to move the weight or load (L). The fulcrum of a lever is the point at which the lever pivots to lift or move a weight; for martial artists, this is the most user-friendly definition.

There are three types of levers in physics, called first-, second- and third-class levers. Each functions differently, but all three can be found in the human body, which is why you need to understand how they work.

In a first-class lever, the fulcrum lies between the effort and the load:

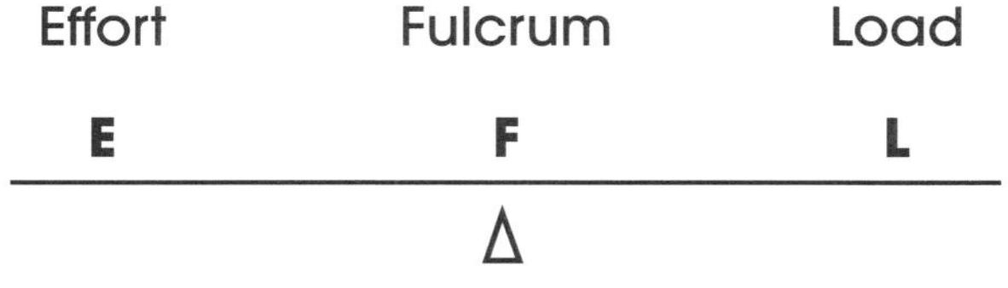

| Effort | Fulcrum | Load |
|---|---|---|
| **E** | **F** | **L** |
| | Δ | |

A first-class lever has the following elements:

**1.** The effort is at one end of the lever.

**2.** The load is at the opposite end of the lever.

3. The fulcrum is between the effort and load.
4. The effort and load move in opposite directions.

Seesaws and water-pump handles are first-class levers. In the human body, tilting the head backward or forward serves as a good example of a first-class lever. The base of the skull acts as the lever, and the joint of the topmost vertebra acts as the fulcrum. The muscles in the front of the neck contract (the effort) and lift the back of the head (the load). The first-class lever is commonly used in judo throws and joint locks.

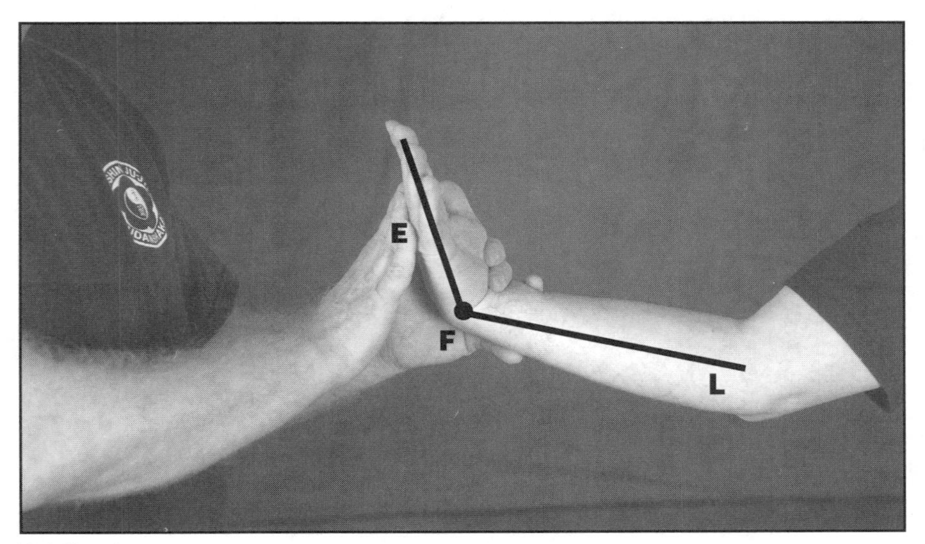

First-Class Lever

In a second-class lever, the load lies between the effort and the fulcrum.

| Effort | Load | Fulcrum |
|---|---|---|
| E | L | F |
| | | Δ |

A second-class lever has the following elements:
1. The effort is at one end of the lever.
2. The fulcrum is at the opposite end.
3. The load is in the middle.
4. The effort and load move in the same direction.

Doors and nutcrackers are second-class levers. In the human body, raising your heel off the ground serves as a good example of a second-class lever. The foot acts as the lever, and the ball of the foot acts as the fulcrum. The calf muscle contracts (the effort) and lifts the body (the load). The second-class lever is used for certain winding and drop-type judo throws and for some chokes.

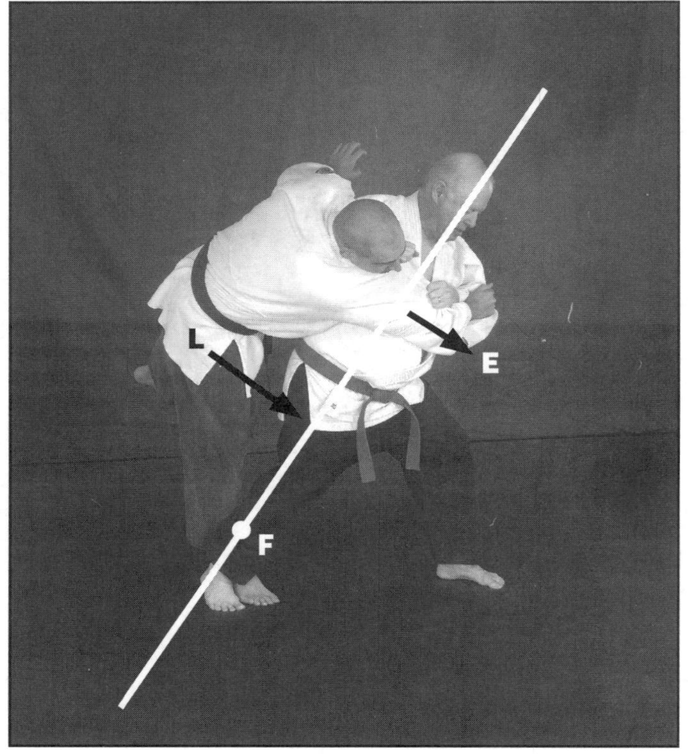


Second-Class Lever

In the third-class lever, the effort lies between the load and the fulcrum:

| Load | Effort | Fulcrum |
|---|---|---|
| **L** | **E** | **F** |
| | | Δ |

A third-class lever has the following elements:

**1.** The load is at one end of the lever.

**2.** The fulcrum is at the opposite end.

**3.** The effort is between the load and the fulcrum.

**4.** The load and the effort move in the same direction.

Forceps and tweezers are third-class levers. This is the most common type of lever found in the human body, most obviously in the elbow and knee. When you bend your arm to lift your hand, your lower arm acts as the lever and your elbow acts as the fulcrum. Your hand acts as the load, and the upper-arm muscles contracting constitutes the effort. When you bend your leg, your lower leg acts as the lever and your knee acts as the fulcrum. Your foot acts as the load, and the contracting of the upper-leg muscles constitutes the effort. This type of lever is usually used to deliver karate strikes and kicks.

Third-Class Lever

In the martial arts, levers can be used in combination for more effective holds, throws and techniques.

The *tai otoshi* starts out as a first-class lever, with the effort at the ankle and the fulcrum at the calf.

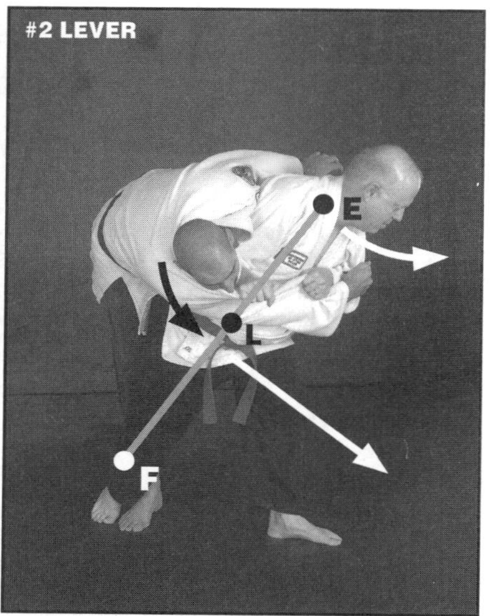


A second-class lever is used to finish the throw. When you turn, the effort switches to your upper body, with the fulcrum at the ankle.

## Joint Rotation

Proper joint rotation is the key to the successful execution of most martial arts techniques. Yes, this even includes the simple wrist and elbow rotations necessary to execute a proper straight punch in karate. Joint rotation can be dealt with superficially: As you execute a straight punch, start with your palm up and make a fist, then turn your fist to a palm-down position as you straighten your arm while shifting your right hip forward just before impact to maximize the force of your punch.

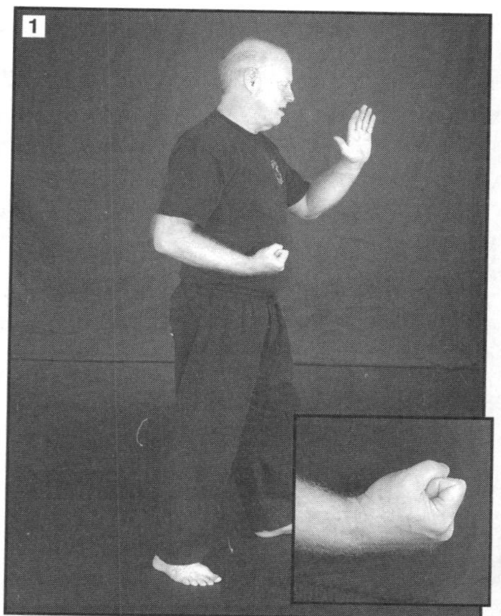


For maximum power, begin with your palm up.

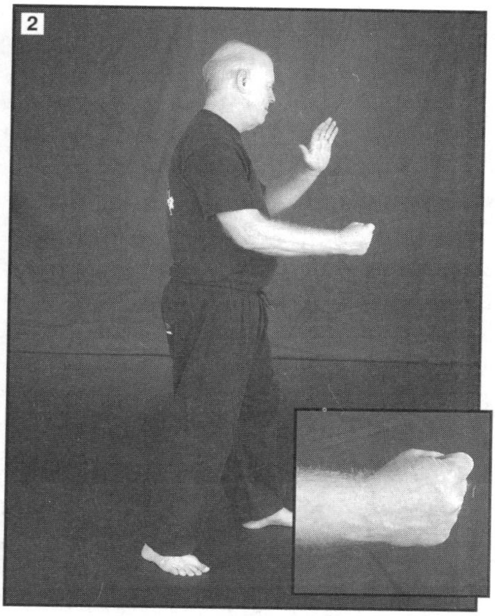

As you strike, rotate your palm.

Just before impact, the fist should be in a palm-down position.

The same concept can be applied to judo when teaching the hip throw *koshi nage*.

Grab your *uke's* right sleeve with your left hand and his left lapel with your right hand.

Pivot in, first with your right foot and then with your left, and raise your right arm under his right arm. Your back is now against him and you're facing the same direction.

With your feet about a shoulder-width apart, squat down while making sure that your right hip is sticking out beyond his right hip.

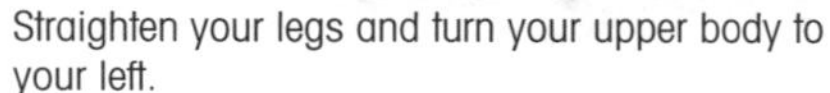
Straighten your legs and turn your upper body to your left.

Throw the uke over your right shoulder.

Both of these are simple explanations that are sufficient for a new student learning basic moves. However, an advanced karate or judo student needs more substantive instruction vis-à-vis joint rotation, different kinds of joints and their limitations, and how proper joint rotation makes techniques effective.

Rotation is the movement of anything—even a body part—around its own axis. Every joint has an x-, y- and z-axis, regardless of how much or how little it rotates. As an example, let's look at the wrist. The y-axis would be visualized as a straight line going through the middle of the hand and up through the middle of the forearm. The x-axis would move with the hand's rotation in relation to the forearm, and the z-axis would move with the forward or backward bending of the hand.

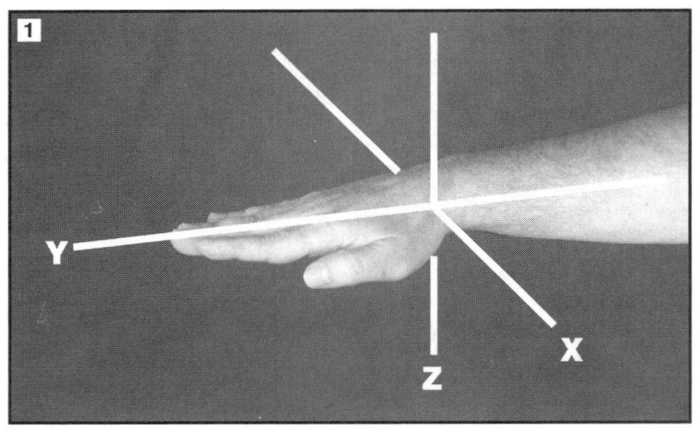


The wrist, like all joints, has its own xyz-axis.

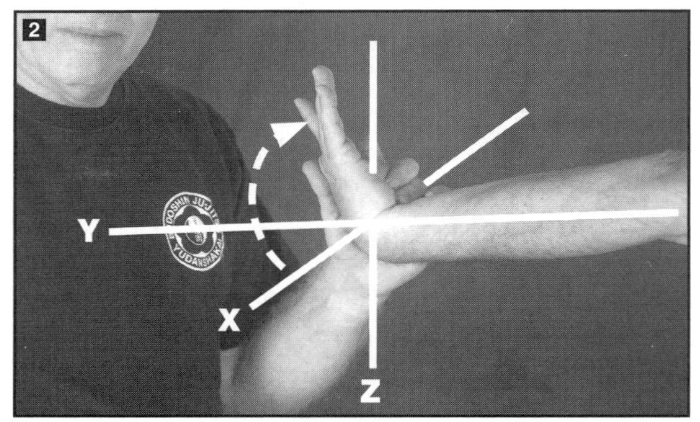


When setting up for a wrist throw (*te nage*), you bend the hand inward on its x-axis.

But we're getting way ahead of ourselves here. As you will see, how joints are manipulated will determine the success of your techniques. Once you have an understanding of kinesthetics, you'll be amazed by how these concepts can be applied to make you a better martial artist.

The human body contains three general types of joints: fibrous, cartilaginous and synovial. Fibrous joints don't move. Examples of fibrous joints include the sutures connecting the different bones of the skull and the sockets that hold the teeth in place. Cartilaginous joints have very limited movement, and examples include the disks between the vertebrae and the cartilage between the sacrum (the lowest part of the spine) and the pelvis.

Last but not least, synovial joints—the most common in the human body—move freely within their structure. The tips of the bones in a synovial joint have a smooth cartilage layer and are surrounded by synovial fluid, which acts as a lubricant, and the joint is held together with ligaments to keep everything in place. There are six types of synovial joints:

| Synovial Joint | Type of Movement | Location |
|---|---|---|
| Ball and Socket | Rotates 360 degrees in all directions<br>Most mobile | Hip<br>Shoulder |
| Hinge | Moves in one plane only<br>Bends and straightens | Knee<br>Elbow<br>Finger<br>Toe<br>Ankle |
| Gliding/Plane | Glides between flat surfaces | Wrist<br>Ankle<br>Vertebrae |
| Pivot | One bone rotates around the axis of another | Forarm rotation<br>Neck (turning left or right) |
| Ellipsoidal | Capable of all types of movement except pivotal<br>Moves in two planes | Wrist<br>Base of Index finger |
| Saddle | Rocks back and forth, moves side to side<br>Limited rotation | Thumb |

The effective use of synovial joints makes the techniques of jujitsu and most other soft martial arts possible, but being familiar with the different types of joints is only half the formula for the effective use of joint techniques. One also needs to understand the concept of joint chains and joint hierarchy.

There's an old camp song called "Dry Bones," which goes: *The hand bone connected to the wrist bone/The wrist bone connected to the arm bone/The arm bone connected to the elbone*. Although it may not be anatomically perfect, the song is relevant because it describes joint chains and joint hierarchy.

A joint chain is a group of linearly connected joints and bones. Visually, this means that you could draw a line through a joint chain without retracing your path. For example, a valid joint chain would go from the index finger through the hand, forearm, upper arm and shoulder. A joint chain contains a parent joint, which is the highest point (the point closest to the head), and the joints descending from the parent joint are known as child joints. This relationship is known as the joint-chain hierarchy. If I raise my hand, forearm, upper arm and the associated joints (the wrist, elbow and shoulder), the joint-chain hierarchy would be shoulder-elbow-wrist.

There are three more elements we need to examine before the joint-chain hierarchy becomes something useful with respect to martial arts techniques. The first element is called "joint resistance" or "dampening." When a joint reaches the limit of its rotational ability, rather than just stopping cold, its resistance increases and its motion tends to slow down. This acts as a natural buffer that prevents joints from locking suddenly or reversing direction. When a joint is at its maximum rotation, it will dampen and not rotate any farther. Joint dampening at one joint will force joint dampening of the other joints in the hierarchy. For example, when I execute a te nage on my opponent, the outward rotation (abduction) of his arm creates sufficient stress to dampen his wrist, elbow and shoulder, forcing his body to turn.

The next element to be considered is the source of orientation of joint chains. The position of a child joint is dependent on its parent joint, and the movement of a child joint generally originates from its parent joint. The last element is called the root joint. Generally, the highest joint in the hierarchy is called the root joint. In the skeletal structure of the human body, this would logically be the joint between the skull and the spine, commonly known as the atlas. The sacrum, however, serves as the base for the entire skeletal structure above and below it. The sacrum is generally considered to be the root joint in the human body because any joint movement can be tracked to it.

As stated previously, when sufficient stress dampens all of your opponent's child joints, the parent joint will move and dampen. If pressure continues to be exerted, it will alter his x- and y-axis and force him to move his atlas, which will force him to move his sacrum and disrupt his center of balance. This is what is actually happening to your opponent's body as you execute a basic hand throw.

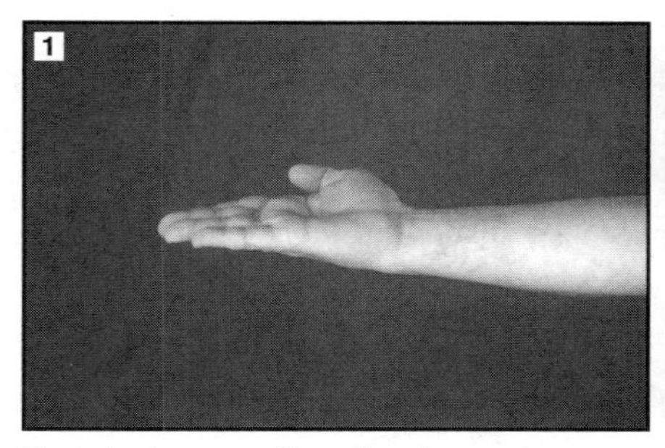


Normal palm-up position of hand.

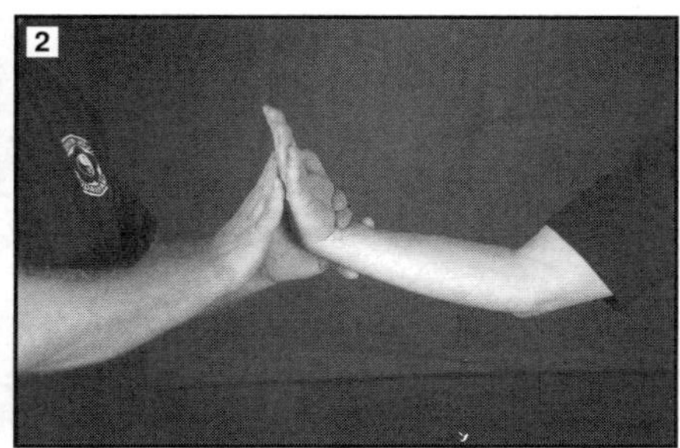


Applying pressure to the x- and y-axis of the hand while bending it slightly outward locks the wrist (the first joint in the joint-chain hierarchy).

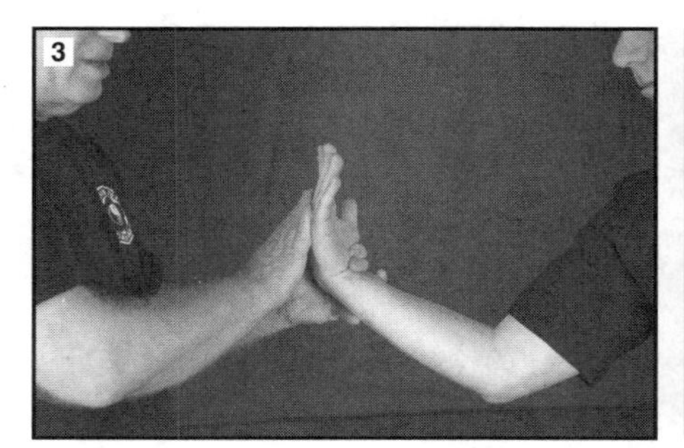


Further pressure causes the elbow to lock, forcing the attacker to begin leaning to his right.

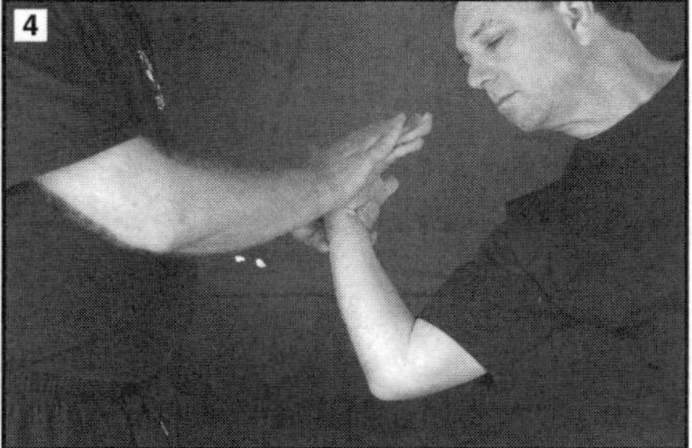


Continued pressure will lock the shoulder, forcing the attacker more off-balance.

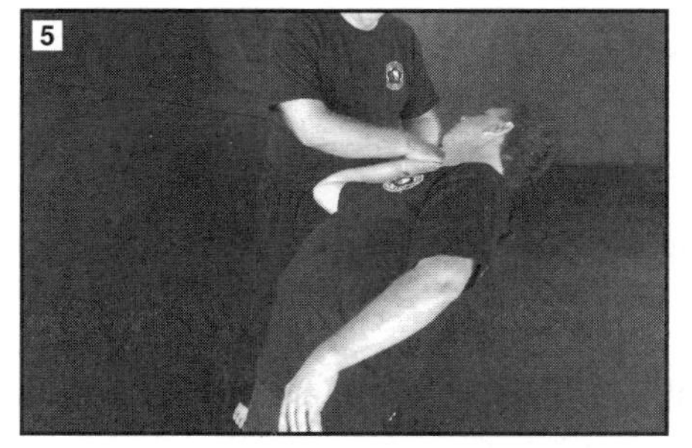


*Te nage* is set with all the joints in the joint hierarchy locked. His sacrum can no longer support his torso, and he will fall backward to the right.

There is a basic rule in judo: Whatever direction the head is going, the body will follow. In the soft arts, the rule is expanded: Your attacker's body will turn in whatever direction his head is turned. In all martial arts, your own body will go in whatever direction your head is turned or facing, which is why sensei always says, "Look in the direction you want to go, not where the attacker is."

## Torque

Have you ever changed a car tire? Ever used one of those short-handled tire irons that come in your tire changing kit? The lugs on your tire were probably tightened with an air ratchet, and you think you're going to loosen them with a tool that maybe has a 12-inch shaft? Get real.

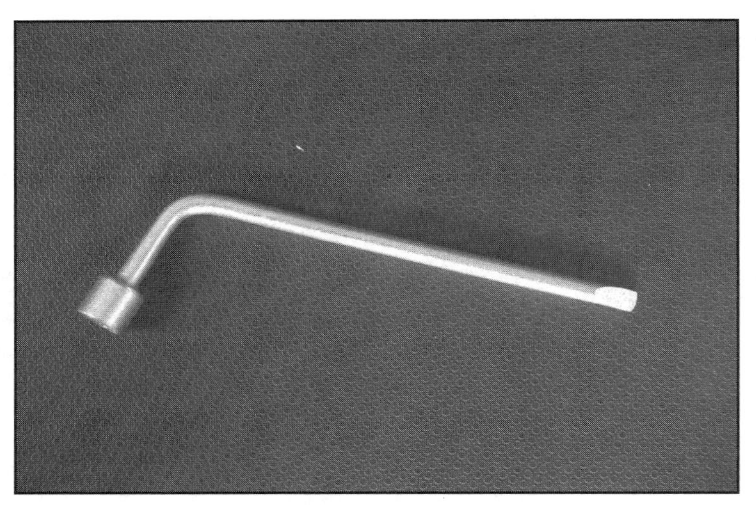

Tire irons are too short to provide enough torque.

The inability to loosen the lug nuts has little to do with strength and more to do with torque. Because you're smart, you also keep a 3-foot-long galvanized pipe in the trunk of your car. (No, it's not there for self-defense purposes.) Simply slide the pipe over the tire iron handle, and it's 3 feet long. The extra length of the handle allows you to deliver sufficient torque to loosen the lug nuts with much less effort.

Scientifically, torque is defined as the force that causes rotation around an axis, and torsion is the actual process of twisting an object around its axis, or the mechanical stress that forces the object to turn. Just as one must understand joint-chain hierarchy in order to understand kinesthetics, one must also understand torque and torsion to understand why joint-chain hierarchies make techniques effective. The body's joints don't just lock up on their own, and sprains, breaks and joint dislocations don't just happen. They're all the result of applying torque. Ligaments, which connect bone to bone, will allow only for a certain amount of movement. As a joint is torqued and reaches its limit, the ligaments cause the turning process to dampen and eventually stop. If torsion is applied to the joint after it has "locked" (reached the limit of its flexibility or rotation), injury to the joint is the only possible outcome.

If you twist the hand of your *uke* in order to throw him, you apply torque to the wrist. As the wrist joint dampens, the torque is transferred up the forearm to the elbow. If the hand is turned quickly, however, the torsion won't transfer in time and the wrist will be sprained or broken. Even if the wrist is injured, in a street situation the elbow and shoulder joints will still lock and the throw can still be successfully executed.

Opposite view of *te nage*. Note the torque created by locking the wrist, elbow and shoulder.

The opponent must go over or risk injury.

The application of the appropriate amount of torque is absolutely essential to the execution of most martial arts techniques, particularly for throws and pain-compliance techniques. For example, if you execute a te nage by placing your thumbs at the base of your opponent's wrist, you will not be able to develop much leverage or resultant torque. However, if you place your thumbs at the base of his knuckles, you will be able to maximize your torque.

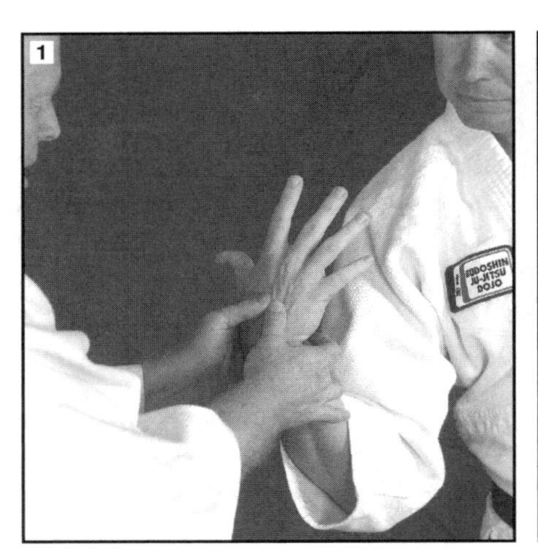


When *te nage* is executed with the thumbs at the base of the hand, there is little leverage or torque.

With the thumbs placed higher on the attacker's hand, at the base of his knuckles, leverage and torque are dramatically increased.

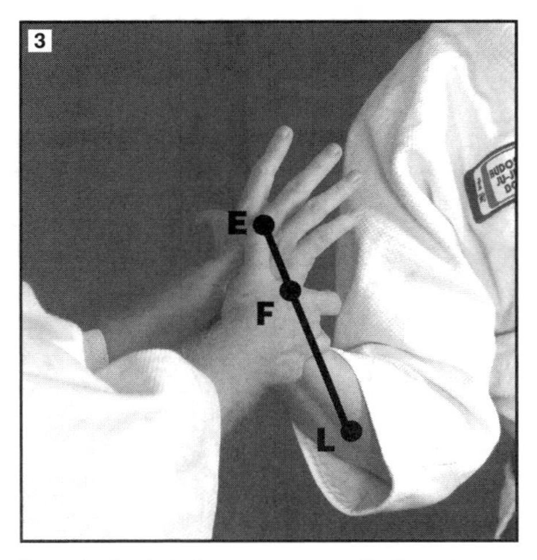


To make the technique even more effective, place the right thumb over the left thumb. This places all the pressure on a single point and creates a first-class lever.

## Motion and Force

Physics and science do not exist in a vacuum, and neither do the martial arts. Most of the material presented thus far has taken place in a static environment. We've been talking about axes, planes, levers and other factors as if they're individual entities. In reality, they do not function in isolation or independently of one another. The action of one element will affect the other; they are codependent for functionality. However, for all of them to function together, there must be motion, and motion requires a sufficient output of energy.

Motion is the movement of a mass (any solid object) from one point to another. Force is the amount of energy required to move the mass from point A to point B. So if we're going to put all these scientific concepts together into something that is really usable, we have to give it movement. In the martial arts, there are three types of force that we need to consider: complementary force, opposing force and circular force. Each type uses ki in a different way.

Complementary force is used in soft arts and soft techniques, when you adjust your axes, levers and planes to blend with those of your opponent. In doing so, you can parallel his motion or superimpose yours over his, redirect his ki in a direction you desire, and use both his and your energy to execute the technique you desire. In essence, you have become one with your attacker. As my sensei put it so many times, "It is always easier to *help* your attacker go where he wants to go." Complementary force can be directed in a circular or linear direction.

An inside sleeve-pull throw is a good example of complementary force in both linear and circular directions.

As the attacker punches, deflect the strike with an outward left block.

continued on next page

Step in with your right foot and grab his right sleeve with both hands.

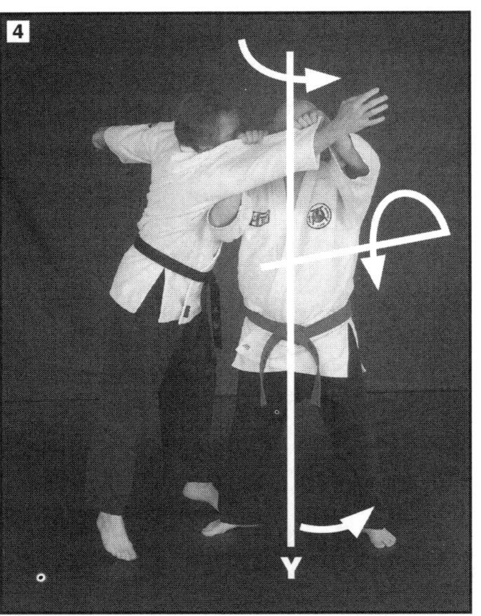


Pull his arm forward and slightly upward, to continue his momentum (his *ki* flow) and off-balance him.

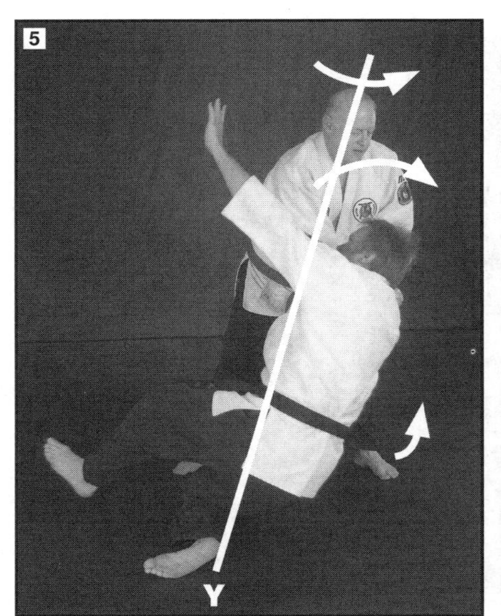


Continue rotating his arm outward and away from you, as if you were rowing a boat, while turning counterclockwise.

If you wish, you can continue pivoting your left foot backward to control his fall and ensure that he falls in front of you. Be sure to continue the circular motion of his arm.

Opposing force is used in hard arts and hard techniques, when the goal is to create an extremely strong base in order to move your opponent back on his z-axis, or to the right or left along his x-axis.

Using a strike against a strike is an example of opposing force.

Block the strike with a hard left outward block.

Step in with your right foot and simultaneously strike him in the sternum with an open palm, destroying his balance. Stepping in also reduces his effective target zone because he will be too close to strike with his left hand. As you move forward, your y-axis changes from $y_{1a}$ to $y_{1b}$ as your attacker's y-axis moves from $y_{2a}$ to $y_{2b}$. The broken line indicates the outer edge of your and the attacker's spheres (or effective *ki* extension.)

A similar technique involves sidestepping.

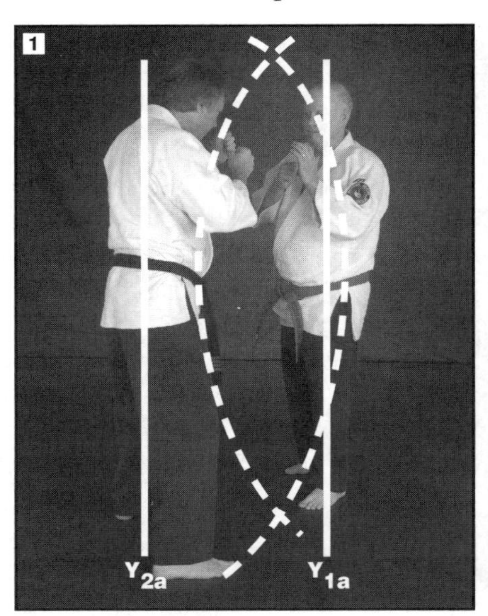


Assume the ready position. (The dotted line indicates the outer edges of you and your attacker's spheres [or effective *ki* extension].)

As the attacker punches, step to the left and slightly forward while deflecting the strike across his body with your right hand. (Your y -axis shifts to the left as you move your body to the left.)

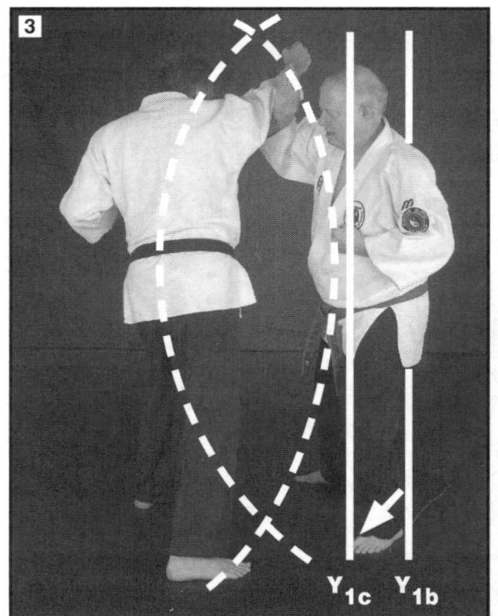


Raise his arm. His entire right side is now open to attack. (Your y-axis moves forward from $y_{1b}$ to $y_{1c}$ as you slide your left foot forward.)

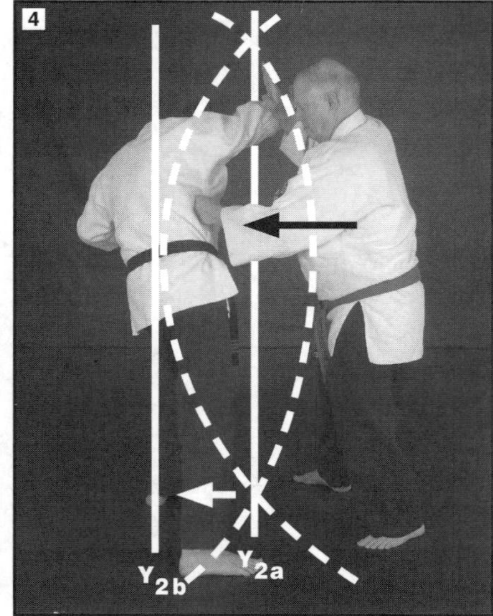


Deliver a straight punch to his floating ribs. (The attacker's y-axis shifts from $y_{2a}$ to $y_{2b}$ as the punch is landed.)

Circular-force techniques tend to be used in soft arts, when the force from an attack is redirected into a circular motion at 90 degrees or greater. All of these concepts can be combined. As the following technique illustrates, a strike blocked with a hard block can be redirected in a circular direction, and the circular force can then be converted to complementary force.

As the attacker strikes, block outward with your left hand.

Step in with your right foot while grabbing his right sleeve with both hands, raising it and rotating it backward.

continued on next page

Continue rotating the arm backward and away from you in a rowing motion.

Bring the arm around to the front of the attacker and begin turning clockwise.

Continue turning while holding the sleeve, bringing the arm around and back.

End with a *guruma ushiro* (shoulder-lock rear takedown).

Even though all three of these forces—or, more correctly, directions of ki—are approached differently, the goal is the same: submit or counter the assailant's attack by controlling his ki. In each case, the attacker's ki is redirected and used against him, causing him to become unbalanced.

## Consequences

So now you have all this theory. You're familiar with axes, planes, leverage, joint rotation and ki. What is its value, practically speaking? What can you do with it?

For every action there is a consequence. If you understand why you're doing something, you'll be able to do it more effectively. Our goal now is to look at some of the areas where all of this theory can be applied. We'll concentrate on off-balancing, pain compliance, impact, and the injuries that result from the effective application of all of the above.

## Off-Balancing

Off-balancing your opponent is essential in a physical conflict. The goal is to remove him from his strong base or secure position—and it can be physical or psychological in nature.

To physically off-balance your opponent, you must use his or your energy to move him into different quadrants and disrupt his secure base. This can be done through the use of leverage, joint-locking techniques, joint rotations, strikes, pressure points or balance-point techniques. Physically off-balancing your opponent is a relatively simple process.

Psychologically off-balancing your opponent is different but can be equally effective. It involves verbal and visual distractions that create doubt in your opponent. Verbal distractions include feigning fear ("Please don't hurt me!"), cooperation ("I'll give you whatever you want!") or continuously talking to your assailant, trying to get him involved in a conversation. The *kiai* is also a verbal distraction because it can be loud and jarring. Visual distractions include holding your hands up with your palms facing outward or handing your attacker what he wants (your keys, wallet, purse, jewelry, etc.) and "accidentally" dropping it at the last moment. More subtle but equally effective visual distractions include moving one or two fingers on one hand, taking your eyes off your assailant as if you're looking at someone behind him, or shifting your body slightly.

Creating doubt in the mind of your opponent is another psychological method of off-balancing. If you look directly into your opponent's eyes, you create doubt because you "ID'd" him. If he looks down or away, you can take advantage of it by executing a technique or escaping. Looking "through" your opponent's eyes can be even more disconcerting because he'll think you're paying more attention to something else. Also, if you stare through his eyes in an unfocused manner, it enhances your peripheral vision and allows you to pick up on any movement around him.

Regardless of which approach you use, off-balancing serves only one purpose. You might think it distracts your opponent or allows you to effectively execute a technique, but these are only byproducts. Your only real goal in off-balancing your opponent is to create a reaction-time gap of 0.3 to 0.7 seconds in his thought pattern, forcing him to react to your actions rather than anticipate them. When you create a 0.3-to-0.7-second reaction gap, he will mentally be at least that far behind whatever you physically do to him. In other words, if you create one distraction after another to keep his mind occupied, it can never catch up with what you are currently doing; you will win because he will be unable to counteract anything you do in a timely manner.

In the following sequence, the reaction gap is increased to the point at which the assailant suffers so much time lag (1.8 to 4.2 seconds) that he simply cannot respond to all that is being done to him, much less counter it. This is why you should never depend on just one technique.

Creating a reaction gap is a critical element in effective self-defense.

As the attacker punches, block outward with your left hand. Note that a hard block can stun the arm if you hit a nerve center.

Step in with your right foot while delivering a back-hand strike to the groin.

As he bends over in reaction to the groin strike, rotate your forearm at the elbow and come up with a back-hand strike to his right cheekbone.

As he reacts to the face strike, step to the outside with your left foot and sweep his right leg.

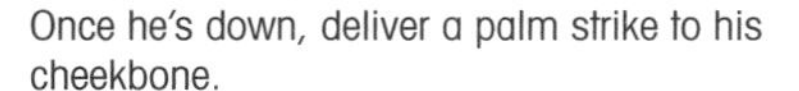

Once he's down, deliver a palm strike to his cheekbone.

Follow the palm strike with a knee drop to his right side.

## Pain Compliance

Pain compliance is a law-enforcement term that involves applying enough pain to a noncompliant suspect to make him cooperate. Pain compliance is not the same as simply creating pain. You can create pain by hitting a person, throwing him on the ground and beating him senseless. But with pain compliance, one avoids injuring the other person because it makes it very difficult to control him.

Pain-compliance techniques have a long history in jujitsu, *aiki-jutsu* and some *ryu* of aikido. In these traditional martial arts, many methods are used to create pain and control assailants, including joint locks, joint manipulations, joint rotations, leverage (levers), and nerve and pressure points (usually combined with off-balancing). Several pain-compliance techniques can be combined for more devastating techniques, like extremely fast submissions that usually result in serious joint injury.

These techniques are taught in many traditional martial arts, and controlling the opponent with the minimal pain necessary for compliance has become the general watchword. To do otherwise would create a rapidly declining student body because of injuries. This also allows students to determine the effectiveness of their techniques by feeling and sensing how their opponents react to them in the dojo. As students practice on each other, they develop an acute physical awareness of how much effort is needed to secure their opponent's compliance.

Clear, assertive verbal commands are another integral part of pain compliance from a modern law-enforcement viewpoint: "Get down. Lie flat. Turn your head. Don't move." These and other simple commands make physical pain-compliance techniques far more effective; they also justify increasing the level of pain if the opponent does not comply with the verbal request.

Another advantage of using pain compliance is that it minimizes the use of force. Although you are entitled to use "reasonable" force while defending yourself, pain-compliance techniques often allow you to use less force than your opponent, reducing the chance of being accused of using "excessive" force—a crime punishable by jail time.

## Impact by Strikes and Throws

In the soft arts, strikes and kicks are usually used as distractions to create a reaction gap to allow the execution of other techniques. Strikes and kicks of this type only need to make contact with the opponent to create the distraction. They do not need to create injury. In contrast, strikes and kicks delivered by hard-art practitioners are themselves the self-defense techniques and, as such, are designed to injure the targeted area.

Throwing an opponent on or against a solid object can also cause serious injury. Skilled defenders can usually control the impact force that the assailant receives based on the situation and the resistance of the attacker. Keep in mind that resistance to any type of soft-art technique ultimately creates more pain, leverage, torque and momentum because the defender is forced to use a greater amount of energy.

## Summary

If you plan to have a thorough understanding of your martial art, you need to get beyond the simple memorization of kata, forms and techniques. Hopefully, this book will help you understand the relationship between martial arts concepts and objective mathematical and scientific concepts in two ways: (1) why techniques work, and (2) that most techniques are based on a relatively few common movements of the human body.

If you can visualize the three axes going through your saiki tanden, you have mastered the most difficult concept in this book. If your techniques are executed properly, the axis lines will be fixed relative to your saiki tanden. How you defend yourself is always dependent on you and your opponent's position with respect to your xyz-axes. For some people, it's easier to visualize the three planes as a sphere.

The ultimate purpose of a block, deflection or verbal response is to distract or "off-balance" your attacker—to create a reaction gap to "get ahead" of his movements.

To understand how techniques work, it is essential to understand levers and how they are applied to martial arts techniques. There are three types of levers: first, second and third class. In the martial arts, levers may be used in combinations to achieve more effective holds, throws and techniques. If you understand the different levers and their locations in the human body, you can execute more effective techniques with less effort.

Proper joint rotation is another key to successful techniques. Joints affect the movement of the rest of the human body. Most joints of the human body are synovial joints. The effective use of synovial joints make the techniques of jujitsu and most other soft martial arts possible.

A joint chain is any group of joints and the attached bones that are linearly connected. As a joint reaches the limit of its rotation, its motion tends to slow down or "dampen." Dampening one joint will force the dampening of the other joints in the hierarchy.

Off-balancing your opponent is essential to success. There is only one purpose for off-balancing your opponent—to create a reaction gap so that he is at a mental and physical disadvantage.

If you have learned your art well and have extensive practice with street simulations, you should be able to defend yourself reasonably well. If you understand the concepts presented in the first part of this book and can apply them to your art and to street situations, you will be able to defend yourself much better. You'll also become an exceptional sensei should you choose such a path.

# PART II: MEDITATION

Martial arts practitioners come and go. They study an art for a few years and then go off and do something else. Some achieve a high level of technical proficiency, open their own dojo for a few years, but succumb to economic or instructional realities and decide to do something else with their lives. There may be a strong commitment to the martial arts, but a tree is only as strong as its roots.

Martial artists are a different breed. They are willing to make a lifelong commitment to achieve technical proficiency as well as a physical and philosophical understanding of their martial art. This will often include a recognition of the validity of all martial arts and an understanding of their similarities, differences, strengths and weaknesses. A martial artist seeks not only to achieve a holistic understanding of the physical aspects of his art (how and why techniques work and their interrelationships) but also to understand how he, as an individual, fits into the scheme of his martial art. He also seeks to develop skills to help bring a sense of peace, calmness and introspection that will help make him a better person, martial artist and sensei. He recognizes that he also represents his art at the philosophical level. The martial artist is the representative of his art, his students, the martial arts community and the human community.

In a word, a martial artist is humble. He can perceive his role in the larger community and recognizes its awesome responsibility. He recognizes the role of his ego and the need for integrity, honesty, fairness and respect for others. To balance all these elements requires the humbleness to seek introspection, to look into oneself, to use some form of meditation to gain insight into his role in the greater scheme of things and resolve conflicts in thinking, and hopefully to discover some "truths" about himself and the world around him. Trust me, this experience can make you humble and bring a new perspective to your life.

You must turn in this direction to grow from a martial arts practitioner to a martial artist. To move to this ultimate growth, you must be able to slow yourself down, isolate yourself from your exterior environment, and give your body, mind and heart time to balance each other. In other words, you need to find a form of meditation that allows you this opportunity.

The ability to meditate is essential to your psychological well-being, and your psychological well-being is essential to your physical well-being. Your psychological and physical well-being are essential to your general well-being. Your general well-being is essential to maintaining an inner calm, which will allow you to deal effectively with the external factors that confront you.

Meditation doesn't just happen. A number of factors can affect your ability to meditate, including your environment, allowable time, technique and goals. You will learn how relaxing your mind can help make you a better martial artist. We will also look at mushin as a form of meditation and its implications to you as a martial artist.

## Environment

Your environment is everything that affects your being, externally and internally. External factors include your physical surroundings, whether you are sitting next to a bubbling brook deep in a forest or standing in the middle of a busy city intersection. Input from your external environment is provided by your five senses: sight, smell, hearing, taste and touch. Your five senses operate at different levels to provide information about your environment. All of these sensors are providing input to your brain as they are stimulated by outside events.

Internal environmental factors are those things that affect your inner being that come from within your body itself. How do you feel physically? Healthy? Sick? Tired? Energetic? How do you feel emotionally? Happy? Sad? Stressed? Relaxed? Mad? Relieved? Secure? Internal environmental factors are also affected by how you interpret the external factors and which ones you concentrate on. All of these internal factors also affect your inner being.

As external and internal environmental factors affect your inner being, your perception of your inner being also affects your outlook toward the environmental factors and your perception of your surroundings and how they affect you. The relationship between your inner self and your environment (external and internal) is cyclical.

Your environment affects your inner being and your inner being affects your perception of your environment. The key word here is "perception." In essence, it could be said that your perception of your environment determines how you interpret your environment.

We are now at a point at which we can ask how meditation affects our environment. Meditation in and of itself cannot change your environment. However, it can affect your perception of your environment. Good meditation skills will allow you to step back from your environment and look at the elements independently and in different relationships. Meditation can also help you clear your mind of all inputs so that you can look at your environment freshly or from a different, objective perspective. If you can change your perception of your environment, perhaps you can make some changes to your environment. Thus, to some extent, meditation can help you control your environment.

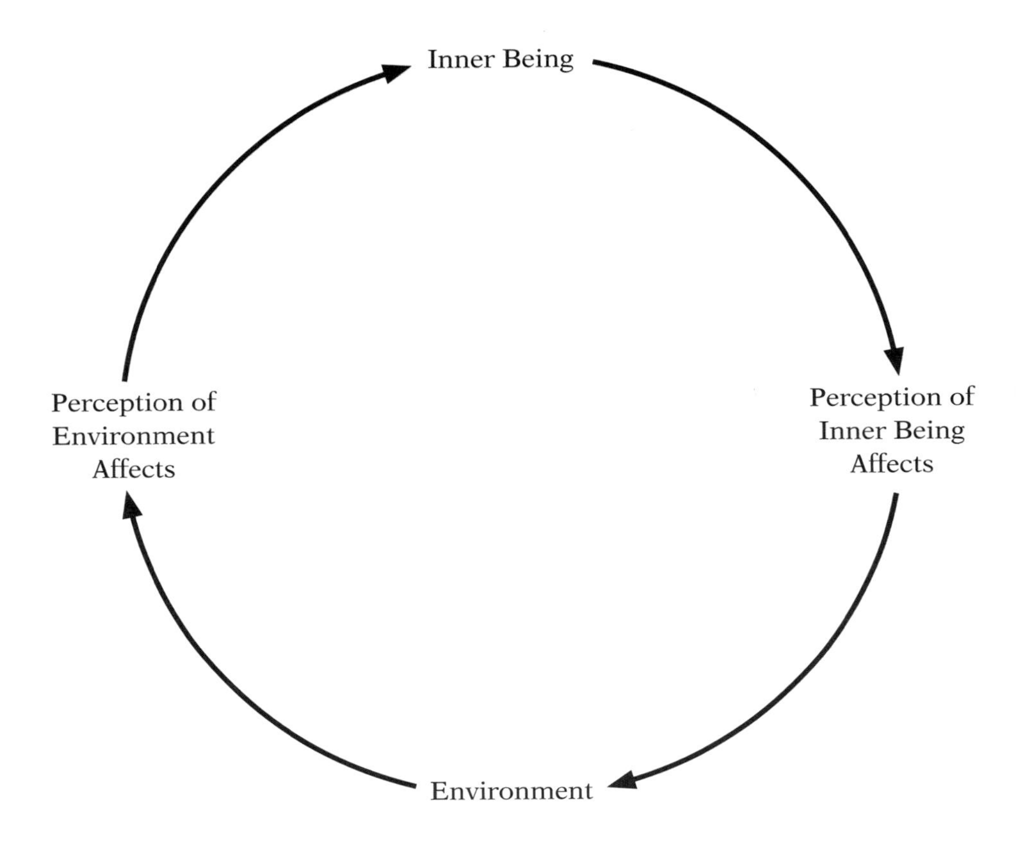


For meditative purposes, your external environment is of critical importance. Most forms of meditation can best be achieved if you are somewhere that is quiet, relaxing and free of distracting stimulation. It should be someplace where you can escape the stress of day-to-day life and secure relaxation and refreshment in your inner being. It might be a softly lit room, a corner of your yard, or a rock you can stand or sit on and overlook the surrounding countryside. Your meditation position should be whatever you're comfortable doing: sitting, standing or lying down. Clothing should be comfortable, loose and relaxed. It is your retreat—a place where you can seek peace for your inner self and put your life and its events in perspective. It is someplace where you can resolve problems or at least gain a different perspective on them that may lead to resolution.

For the martial artist, an awareness of your external environment is critical to your survival. Your senses must be attuned to what is going on around you. Your mind must be open and relaxed to avoid potential situations, if possible, and be able to quickly assess and act on situations in which conflict may result. This is sometimes called the sixth sense. This is not paranoia. Paranoia exists when you are afraid of your environment because you fear what might happen. Being paranoid also increases your chances of being a victim because your visual signals to others indicates fear. Using your sixth sense allows you to anticipate what might potentially happen and either avoid it or establish a plan of action, and then go on with your life. Your sixth sense will enhance your awareness of your external environment, make it possible to avoid unsafe conditions and, most important, prepare you psychologically for the immediate situation.

Rather than projecting a sense of fear, you can present a sense of control that, in and of itself, may reduce the chances of a confrontation or conflict. To do this successfully, you must be inwardly calm while being completely aware of your external environment. By using all your senses, you will use your sixth sense to establish situational awareness.

## Time

Time is a second factor to consider in the meditative process. How much time do you need to meditate? How much time will you have to meditate? When can you meditate? How often can you (or do you need to) meditate? These are all questions you need to consider, and there are no set answers.

The time you need to meditate is determined by several factors. What kind of meditation techniques will you engage in? Do certain environmental conditions need to be in place before meditating? How experienced are you in the particular meditative techniques you are using?

Some self-relaxation techniques take only a few seconds to accomplish (in almost any environment) and can serve to relieve stress or relax or refocus your mind. Some techniques may take a few minutes to place you into a meditative state, depending on how deep you want your meditative level to be. If you are new to a particular meditation technique, it may take 20 to 30 minutes to get into a meditative state, or you may not get there at all on your first few attempts. However, if you are patient with yourself, you will be successful.

The ease of finding an environment conducive to meditation will also affect the meditation time available to you. If that softly lit room is easily accessible, then you can use your time more effectively. If, on the other hand, you have to walk or drive a distance to get to your spot, then the travel time can be a negative or positive factor in the meditation process. If the distance you have to travel is relaxing, such as a walk from one part of your room to another or a short hike up a lush, cool, shaded canyon with a bubbling creek, you can use it to help prepare you for your meditation or to reflect on your meditation. On the other hand, if you have to drive through rush-hour traffic or if you have to deal with your arguing children on the way to or from your place of retreat, the travel to or from your place of retreat can completely undermine the value of your retreat.

By the way, if you've never participated in a professionally run retreat, whether it is religious or philosophical, you are missing out on a great experience. To be able to go to a relaxing and peaceful place you haven't been, have all your material needs taken care of (shelter and meals) and be able to spend one to two or more days securing enlightenment, reflection and introspection on a particular topic where everyone's thoughts are valued and respected—is an opportunity to develop tremendously valuable skills that will help you through any meditation process. Regardless of the retreat topic, with professional guidance you will learn a great deal about yourself, your values and your perception of your environment.

Everyone needs time to reflect, contemplate, reason things out and seek solutions from within. It's even healthy to argue with yourself because that may raise issues and solutions you wouldn't think of otherwise. However, as someone once told me, if you constantly lose arguments with yourself, you really do need professional help (counseling) because there may be serious self-confidence or image issues that need to be resolved.

As a martial artist, it is very important to use different meditation skills for different time frames and situations. Being able to empty your mind quickly so you can deal with a critical situation—whether it is avoiding a traffic accident, defending yourself, making a quick analysis of a business situation or doing what is necessary to save another person's life—is an admirable and commendable skill in any stressful situation. It can save your life. It can allow you to sense your opponent and instantly change the techniques you're using to deal with his resistance or counters. An empty mind can work incredibly fast.

Additionally, other meditation techniques that may require longer time periods can be used for refocusing purposes. Resolving problems, reducing pain or discomfort levels, and relaxing can be accomplished with lengthier meditation.

## A Few Seconds

Depending on how much time you have, there are different activities you can use for meditation or relaxation. If you only have a few seconds to relieve yourself from stressing out or to refocus, your method of relaxation will probably be physical. From shortest to longest period of time, your actions can range from a yawn, a primal scream (do it in a closed room or with no one else in hearing range) or a few slow deep breaths (in the nose, fill the lungs and stomach, exhale through the mouth) to stretching your body or doing an isometric exercise, all the way to closing your eyes and either gently rubbing both temples, using an eye-ridge pressure sequence or imagining yourself someplace else (daydreaming).

All of these "quickie" techniques are fairly self-explanatory, except for the eye-ridge press. The eye-ridge process is relatively simple to put into several steps and can be easily learned:

1. Sit on the ground or in a chair.
2. Rest your head in your hands, with your jawbone resting on your thumbs. Your elbows can rest on a table or desk, if you're sitting at one.
3. Gently close your eyes and leave them gently closed. If you wear glasses, remove them. Contact lenses need not be removed.
4. Press your middle fingers gently against the upper ridge right next to your nose. Your right middle finger will be used for your right eye ridge and your left middle finger for your left eye ridge. Maintain this gentle pressure for a couple of seconds and then remove the pressure.
5. Move your fingers about one-quarter of the way out along the ridge (you might feel a slight notch). Press gently for a couple of seconds and then remove the pressure.
6. Move your fingers to about halfway out along the ridge (you might feel another slight notch). Press gently for a couple of seconds and then remove the pressure.
7. Move your fingers to almost all the way out along the ridge, just past the edge of the eye, where you might feel another slight notch. Press gently for a couple of seconds and then remove the pressure.
8. Place your middle fingers on your temples and either apply gentle pressure for a few seconds or gently rotate your thumbs on your temples a few times toward the front of your head.

9. Place your fingers on the side of your head just in front of the cartilage at the middle of your ears. Press gently for a couple of seconds and then remove the pressure.
10. Place your fingers on the side of your head just in front of the base of your ears. Press gently for a couple of seconds and then remove the pressure.
11. Repeat this process once or twice, and you're done.

It's much nicer to have someone else doing this to you from above your head while you're lying down comfortably on your back, but this sequence is an excellent alternative in terms of self-relaxation. It can work quite well to refocus or relax yourself if you've got a minute.

## Five to 60 Minutes

Generally, the more time you can devote to meditation and relaxation techniques, the more effective they are. The time range of five to 60 minutes (or longer, if needed) can really help to refocus, relax and re-energize yourself, depending on your need. Most meditation techniques fall into this time frame.

Doing meditation in a sitting position on the floor is the ideal position. Sitting in *seiza* (formal sitting position) is the ideal sitting position for some forms of meditation. In seiza, you are sitting on your knees/calves

Formal *seiza* position.

with your feet turned inward. Your back is straight, you're facing forward, your forearms rest on your thighs and your palms are down. For those who cannot sit in seiza on *tatami* or a hard floor for any length of time, there are cushions and "seiza benches" that can help make this a more comfortable experience.

Sitting in seiza for a long time can put your legs to sleep because of the lack of circulation. Although this is not my favorite position for meditation or for formal events in the dojo, there are two things you can do to improve circulation. First, rather than keep your feet straight, turn them inward so you're resting on the outside sides of your feet. Second, cross your big toes. Although this may sound odd, the only rationale I can think of for crossing the big toes is that it helps assure that your feet are turned inward, thus enhancing circulation.

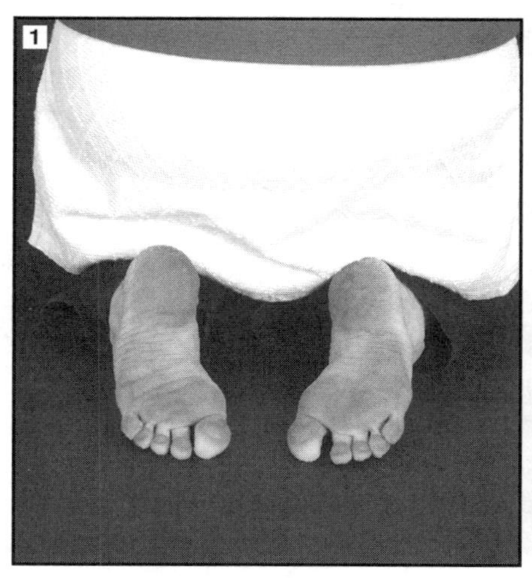


If you sit in the *seiza* position too long with your feet straight out behind you, circulation will be cut off and your feet will fall asleep.

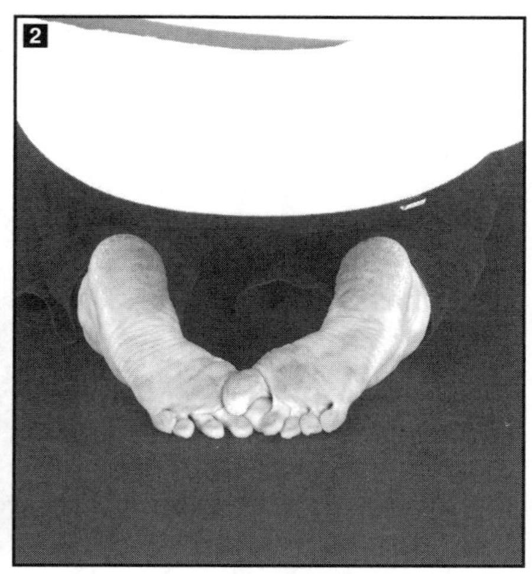


Simply by crossing your big toes, you can sit more comfortably and your feet will retain better circulation.

A less formal version of the seiza used in most traditional martial arts dojo has you sitting with your legs slightly apart (for balance) and your forearms resting across your thighs. Your feet are straight back. Once both of your knees are down, your toes extend back so that you're also resting on your insteps rather than your toes and the balls of your feet. Unfortunately, straightening out your toes so that you're resting on your insteps is not an ideal (or even sound) position for moving into self-defense techniques from a sitting position. (Having your big toes crossed is even worse.)

Sitting cross-legged is another alternative, as is sitting in a chair or lying down. What is important is that you are comfortable so that your meditation position will help you succeed at whatever meditative technique you use. If you have several minutes to meditate, you can engage in centering, focusing, body awareness, projection and visualization. Different types of meditation have different goals, or perhaps it would be more accurate to say no goals at all. For it is in achieving emptiness that you achieve openness and self-realization.

Some people find that a good massage or listening to relaxing music facilitates meditation. Others find that a good workout gives them time to "think." At the very least, a good physical workout may cause the brain to release a significant amount of endorphins that can relieve stress, reduce pain and give one a feeling of euphoria. It should also be noted that, at the other end of the activity spectrum, a good massage can also cause the brain to release endorphins. However, the release of endorphins is not necessarily the same as the euphoria that can be achieved with good meditation.

## One Day or Two

If you've got a day or more during which you can "escape from the world," you can get into even longer-term meditation, although you will probably also be involved in other activities that support your meditative process. Getting out of town for a day or two, going camping or fishing, reading a good book, doing yard work or even painting a room can give you several opportunities for reflection or to seek solace from everyday challenges in your life.

In essence, what you're doing is giving yourself time to think about something while engaging in an activity that in and of itself does not require much, if any, conscious thought—sort of like being in a state of mushin. The statement "I've got to get away from it all" really takes on a sense of legitimacy. After all, if you do something for one or two days that doesn't require much thinking but allows you to gain insight into yourself or a problem you're facing, you're engaged in meditation, whether you realize it or not. And that's one of the major characteristics of meditation—it ideally isn't a conscious effort. Insight will flow when the time is right—when you are relaxed.

## Meditation Techniques

If you have several minutes or longer to meditate, you can engage in a variety of different types of meditation. Although spokespeople for each type of meditation (or particular style within each general category) will probably state that the type of meditation they practice is the best, there is no single best form of meditation (much like there is no "best" martial art). Ultimately, the best meditation method is the one that works best for you. The major types of meditation techniques we'll consider are breathing, centering, body awareness, projection, focusing, relaxation, visualization and contemplation.

## Breathing

Before we look at the different types of meditation, we need to look at a common factor essential to the success of all of them: breathing. Obviously, breathing is essential to life. However, we all breathe differently. Some people inhale and exhale continuously. Others pause a few seconds between each breath. Joggers and swimmers will establish a breathing pattern that is synchronized to their pace of activity. Martial artists will exhale as they execute a technique, thus synchronizing their ki with their physical output. Sometimes just taking a deep breath and exhaling will allow us to refocus on an issue.

Calm, relaxed breathing is essential to success in every form of meditation. Every form of meditation requires that you center and calm yourself. Once you are seated comfortably, you need to slowly and gently close your eyes and take a deep breath. Inhale slowly through your nose, filling up your lungs and stomach. Hold your breath for one to two seconds, and exhale slowly through your mouth until all the air is exhaled. Wait a comfortable amount of time (up to a few seconds) and repeat the process. Do this three to four times.

Do not do this more than three to four times. Even though this process will help you relax, you are also oxygenating your blood much like a sports enthusiast would at the start of a race or other competitive event. Taking more than three to four deep breaths can over-oxygenate your blood, causing you to feel lightheaded or even faint. Neither of these consequences are conducive to meditation (or competing). Once you have completed this initial breathing exercise, you can return to a normal relaxed breathing pattern—again, whatever is comfortable for you.

## Centering

Centering is the process of emptying your mind of everyday thoughts. Although it can be a form of meditation on its own, it also serves as a first step in most of the other meditation techniques covered in this book. For lack of a better phrase, you're becoming familiar with your self. The first step is to exclude external factors. As a thought from the outside enters your mind, you should attempt to let it go and not give it any more effort.

Once you have purged your mind of external thoughts, your next step is to deal with thoughts from your internal environment. As a thought comes to mind, you can think and reflect on it and let it go. A slight variation of this is when you allow a thought to enter your mind as you inhale and exit your mind as you exhale. This process is continued until you've purged all thoughts from your mind and it is ready to explore new thoughts and ideas.

A variance of this concept is when you simply let thoughts enter and leave your mind at will, exploring them if you wish and then letting them go. By letting thoughts come and go as they please, you can either explore them or resolve the issues, putting them to peace. Allowing thoughts to come and go at will relaxes your mind and then your body.

In either case, your goal is to vacate your mind so that you can balance your mind with your hara, or center point. This is a process of emptying your mind so that you can feel your center without any distractions. Once this is achieved, your mind is clear, your body is relaxed and you can be one with yourself and at peace.

## Body Awareness

Another type of meditation is body awareness. The goal of body awareness is simply to become aware of your body by excluding external and internal stimulants to your body. However, rather than concentrating on excluding these elements, your goal is to get a sense of your entire physical body and thereby achieve a sense of relaxation and oneness with your body. Because body-awareness meditation is more proactive than centering, it can be used to reduce or relieve symptomatic pain in some cases.

The theory behind using body-awareness techniques for the relief of pain is really pretty simple. When part of your body is in pain, you think about it. The more you think about it, the more the concept of pain becomes ingrained in your brain. As a result, your brain concentrates on the part of your body that is in pain (or in the most pain) and forgets about everything else. This is why doctors advise their patients to take pain medication as soon as possible after an injury to their body (from an accident or surgery). The rationale is that the pain medication will prevent the brain from establishing a higher level of pain, which is more difficult for pain medication to treat without a higher dosage.

While on vacation a few years ago, I tripped down several stairs (I'm glad I'm not so klutzy in the dojo). The only pain I felt was to my left knee, on which I couldn't put any weight. Two days later, my doctor immobilized my knee with a brace, thus relieving the intensity of the pain. It was only at that point that I realized I had also sprained my right ankle, which had to be taped. I hadn't noticed the pain before that time. As I hobbled out of the hospital on crutches, I was re-educated about the concept that whatever part of the body hurts the most will get the brain's attention.

Body-awareness techniques follow the same logic. Because our brains will naturally concentrate on a particular pain or discomfort, by retuning the brain in to the rest of the body, the level of pain may be reduced or eliminated.

A case in point: Early in my martial arts career, I was heavily involved in backpacking. I was an associate adviser to a coed explorer post that specialized in high-altitude backpacking. We'd usually start at 6,000 to 8,000 feet and go up. One of the problems of high-altitude backpacking is altitude sickness, caused by the thinner oxygen. The physical consequences were either nausea or a headache during the first day. At higher altitudes, regular medications could not be used. Aspirin, which normally reduced headaches by constricting blood vessels or thinning blood, would only aggravate a headache brought on by a lack of oxygen. Constricted blood vessels or thinned blood simply brought less oxygen to the brain. Although we had prescription painkillers in our first-aid kit (most adults had advanced first-aid training, mountaineering first aid, or both), such medications were saved for emergencies. You might think we'd just have to tough it out the first night.

No way! Fortunately, one of the adults knew a number of body-awareness techniques. He taught us two very simple techniques to reduce or eliminate pain. The first one could be self-administered, and it was very easy to teach and not too difficult to master. It actually involves very few steps, as you will see. For the instructional sequence, you need someone else to help you just one time. After that, you can do the entire exercise on your own.

Lie down on a level surface. Make sure your feet are not higher than your head. All clothing should be loose (no shoes or socks). Your palms should face up. Close your eyes.

The other person will lightly touch each of the following areas for a second or two, left or right side first:

1. Tips of toes on one foot, from little to big toe
2. Inside and then outside of ankle
3. Inside and then outside of knee
4. Outside of hip joint
5. Repeat for other leg
6. Tips of fingers on one hand, from little finger to thumb
7. Middle of palm
8. Base of hand at wrist
9. Inside and outside of elbow
10. Tip of shoulder
11. Base of neck at shoulder
12. Repeat on other arm

On your own, without assistance, concentrate on feeling the little toe of one foot until you feel it. Think about the toe next to it while continuing to think of the little toe. Continue this sequence all the way up one leg, keeping all the points that were touched in mind. Do the same for the other leg, and then for each arm, starting at the fingertips.

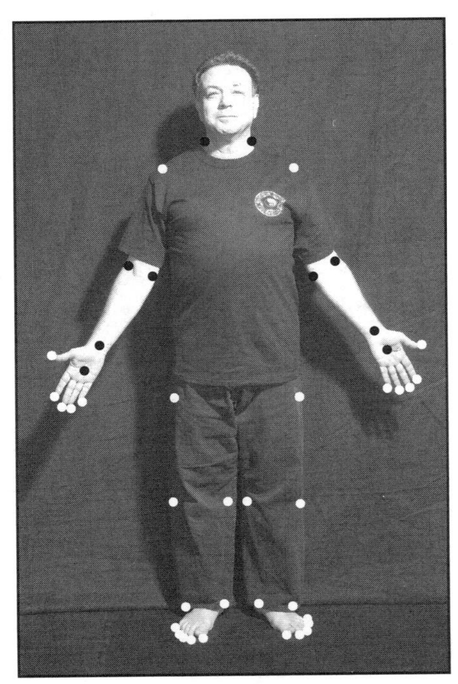

Areas of the body on which to concentrate for the relaxation exercise.

By the time you finish this process, you will be in touch with your entire body and will have a sense of relaxation. Surprisingly, the pain or discomfort will also be greatly reduced or eliminated. There's only one more rule for this activity: If you lose contact with any one point during the exercise, you will need to start over. How long does this exercise take? The first time you try it, it will take about 20 to 30 minutes to finish. Once you get the process down, it should take about five minutes to reconnect with your entire body. From that point, it's very easy to fall asleep.

Although this technique worked well at high altitudes, I never tried it for any other situation until several years later when I developed severe abdominal pain when I tried to go to sleep at night. I went to my doctor, who prescribed a muscle relaxant that worked quite well. However, he also told me that nothing was wrong with me physically and that the problem was probably between my ears. I had a choice of seeking "professional" help or seeing what I could do on my own. I remembered the technique I had learned from my backpacking days and tried it. Although it took a few weeks, I was able to eventually manage the pain, get off the medication and get rid of the stomach discomfort altogether. To this day, I have no idea what the problem was between my ears.

I make a point of teaching this technique in my dojo once every year or so. It's neat watching your whole class put itself to sleep within 15 or 20 minutes. I've done this successfully with classes of adults and junior high-school students. How do you wake them up? The proper way to wake a person up is with a slight touch on the arm or shoulder. I prefer the shoulder.

A second technique he taught to reduce or eliminate a headache that has just started always requires another person but works on the same concept.

Have the person sit comfortably in a chair or on the floor. If he's sitting on the floor, kneel down next to him, facing him, and bring the inner part of your right or left leg up so that it will support his back. If you're left-handed, as I am, this exercise is easier to do if you're on your partner's right side. Have him relax.

**1.** Gently place your left hand at the back base of his skull.

**2.** Gently place your right hand on his forehead.

**3.** Apply constant pressure with both hands—just enough so he can feel it. You're not trying to squeeze his brains out.

**4.** With your hand on the base of his skull, push slightly upward toward his forehead, while the other hand presses the forehead. Use equal pressure with both hands.

**5.** After 30 to 60 seconds, let go quickly with both hands. The headache should be reduced or gone.

All that is happening here is that the person with the headache starts thinking about the pressure from your hands rather than the headache. The pressure is redirecting the person's thoughts so he doesn't think about the headache. If you don't think about something, it won't bother you as much. Please be aware that this technique will not work on a person who's had a headache for some time, because awareness of it has been etched into the person's brain.

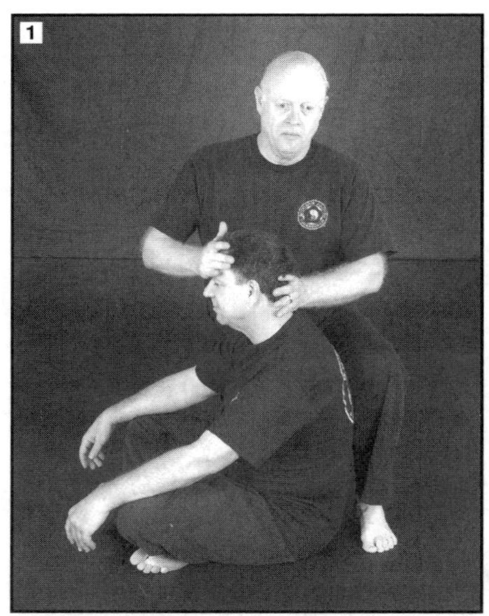

You can have your subject sit in a chair or on the floor with his back against one of your knees.

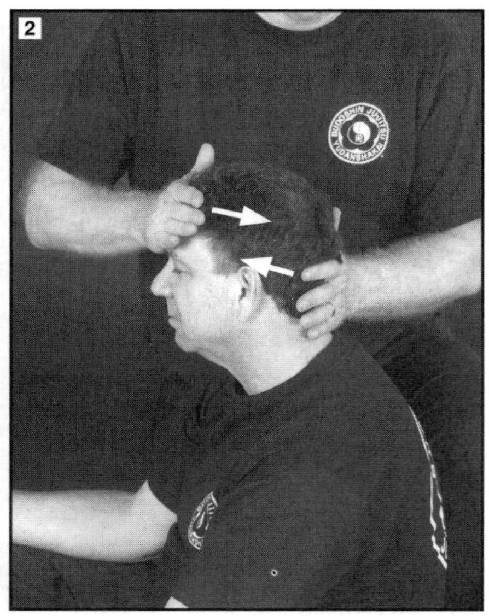

Moderate pressure is applied to both the forehead and the base of his skull. Pressure from the forehead should be directed slightly downward, and pressure from the rear skull base should be directed slightly upward, so both hands are pressing toward each other. A lot of pressure is not needed for this; too much pressure can be counterproductive.

The goal of body-awareness techniques is to get you in touch with your physical being. Although it is a more active approach compared to centering, the goal is the same: to clear your mind, to clear your body and to clear yourself.

## Projection

For some people, centering and body awareness are adequate goals of meditation. The ability to get in touch with one's thoughts and feelings and the ability to cast them off and savor the simple beauty of peace are sufficient rewards and serve to relax the practitioner from the day-to-day tensions of the real world. Some people like to take this process one step further.

One way of doing this is with projection. Projection does what it says it does. You can project your self outward from your body to somewhere or something else. We all used to do this as kids. It was called playing, imagining, pretending, role-playing or a variety of other terms. We used to project ourselves into imaginary situations and act them out either physically or in our imaginations.

Then something happened: We "grew up." We became "adults." We assumed "responsibilities." We became "mature." Simple, innocent thoughts were left behind as the reality of adulthood and earning a living, raising kids, and seeking success and promotion became our goals. A person's success was now measured by "success," with a variety of criteria and measurements. What was lost in most adults was priceless: the mind's ability to feel free and wander where it wished. It was lost so that we could function in the regimented world of adulthood. Is it too great a price to pay?

With projection, you don't have to "pay the price." Your imagination still works. You just need to set your mind free so you can use it. Projection is not too different from creative imagining; to work well, both require that your mind be free from other thoughts, and both require that your mind be completely relaxed and passively open to new ideas or different ways of interpreting information.

Hypothetically, perhaps a Shaolin priest in ancient China, in a state of being centered, inadvertently observed the actions of a crane seeking a meal in a stream. By being in a state of total relaxation, he was able to observe the movements of the crane in such a way to learn its natural movements and apply those concepts to a particular style of martial art he had studied. Perhaps the movements of the crane gave him insights into areas he had never thought of before. Thus, a whole new world was opened based on a single, unanticipated experience.

Projection is the ability to passively look at things differently from a relaxed state of mind. It is the ability to take note of something from an unanticipated perspective because your mind is free to accept new ideas or interpretations. It is your mind's ability to then take these ideas and freely interpret them in a manner that hopefully makes sense while being in a relaxed, centered state. Perhaps this is where the phrases "think outside the box" and "out on a limb" come from.

## Focusing

Focusing is similar to projecting, except that the relaxed mind isn't totally free to wander. The body has to be centered, but a quiet environment is not required. Rather, the goal of focusing is to give some thought to a particular issue. There are two different ways to focus: the Western perspective and the Eastern perspective.

The Western perspective operates on the premise of concentration. If you think about a particular problem or issue long and hard enough, you will find the solution. It's the good old Puritan work ethic: The harder you work, the better person you'll be. The harder you try, the better your chances of success. Unfortunately, working harder or trying harder is no guarantee of success or even mediocrity. All it means is that you have a better chance of wearing yourself out. Working or trying "smarter" is a better alternative, but even that is not a guarantee of success.

The Eastern view looks at focusing quite differently. Once you are centered, you rely on how your body feels with respect to an issue. Rather than concentrating with a specific goal in mind, you allow your body to explore an issue as a process. Rather than try harder, the eastern approach contends that if you're relaxed and don't try to find a solution, you are more inclined to find a solution because your mind and body are free to pursue whatever path or paths they choose.

There are several steps in the Eastern type of focusing. First, you look at the problem mentally to objectively assess the pros and cons. The next step is to look at the issue from an emotional viewpoint. What do you feel is right or wrong (both might be subjective value statements), and what are the issues at this level? What would you be happy or unhappy about? What could you live with? What would you object to? The third step is to consider how various decisions affect you physically. How would you feel? Good? Bad? Indifferent? Mad? Joyous? There is a whole range of feelings that can be considered and weighed.

Last and most important, after going through all of the above steps, what is your gut feeling? This feeling comes out of your hara, or center point. Is your hara comfortable with a particular position, or does it leave you feeling unbalanced, unsure or irritated? You will reflect on the issue as long as necessary, even while conducting the normal affairs of the day, until you come to some resolution where your hara is balanced and you feel that your decision is right. The focusing process can take moments or it can take days. It depends on your ability to refocus yourself as necessary to deal with the issue until a decision is made that leaves your ki balanced.

Focusing can have many positive results in your daily life. It can lead to improved interpersonal relations because you will be better able to discuss your feelings and how you come to decisions. Focusing can result in improved nonjudgmental concentration and problem solving because you will not be out to prove a particular point or prove that you're right. You will look at all the information from a variety of perspectives so that your decision will be better balanced. Last, focusing tends to make you more present-oriented than past-oriented. Rather than wishing things were the way they were before, you realize that you can't go back. You have to accept the past and move forward. Your ability to move forward successfully is based on your ability to look at and evaluate all the information at your disposal so that you can make the right decision for the present and hopefully for the future.

As a martial artist, the ability to focus can affect your sense of mushin. The ability to relax your mind so your body can respond automatically to an attack is a result of an extremely fast focusing ability. There's a gut feeling that you're in a potentially dangerous situation, and you have to know what your options are—fast.

How often have you acted on a gut feeling, and that gut feeling turned out to be right? Amazingly, gut feelings, achieved through a focusing process, have a high success rate at being correct decisions. Sometimes when you make a decision, it's based on a gut feeling rather than on an objective reason. Those decisions usually turn out to be the right ones. Why? Because if you've done enough focusing exercises, you will tend to trust your gut feeling. You will also realize that, because being objective is part of the focusing process, your gut feelings might have an objective base. As you get more experienced with gut feelings, you will become more comfortable with them. However, gut feelings do not arise out of thin air. They are the result of the several steps that can occur in succession quite quickly in a dangerous situation. How quickly they occur depends on your clarity of mind, awareness of your environment and the options open to you. In terms of a street self-defense situation, this is what it comes down to: your gut feeling.

## Common Characteristics

All forms of meditation have common characteristics and will improve your self-confidence and sense of humility. It could be said that "to know your self is to understand yourself." By meditating, you will gain insight into what you think, how you think and your values. You will gain insight into what your body and mind are capable of and also what your limitations are. Being aware of these things—knowing yourself—can help you become more confident. Being able to express your thoughts and feelings may also increase other people's respect for you. Being aware of your limitations and strengths can also make you more humble because you realize you do not need to prove yourself to others.

Meditation helps make you more aware of you and your environment. You will be more in tune with what is occurring in your external environment (surroundings) and your internal environment (feelings). Awareness of your environment is critical to your ability to succeed in that environment (or to alter it, if possible).

Meditation increases your ability to handle crises. You are trained to relax your mind and body. Relaxing your mind is essential to remaining rational, objective and receptive to coming up with viable solutions. A relaxed mind also reduces the level of adrenaline in your body that will raise your stress level beyond what is controllable. A relaxed mind can more quickly direct the body how to act, and the body will cooperate more effectively. Meditation also helps you be more objective because it allows you to look at the same problem, issue or crisis from many different perspectives. Objectivity is essential to good "gut" decisions. It allows you to quickly analyze an issue and come up with a viable solution.

All of the benefits of meditation are of tremendous value to the serious martial artist. The skills learned from meditation can directly improve your ability to quickly move into a state of mushin in critical situations. In his writings, the great swordsman/philosopher Yagyu Munenori said meditation is using your eyes (observation) and your mind (intuition and perception) to achieve understanding and awareness.

## Relaxation

Being relaxed allows your sixth sense to function at its maximum level. Students can practice two training exercises to improve their awareness, both of which are designed to help you sense another person's ki. In the first exercise, sit up straight—either in seiza or in a more comfortable position—facing your partner, with your knees almost touching his. He rests his palms on his thighs and closes his eyes. When he is relaxed, he raises his hands with his palms facing each other, about six inches apart. You then move one hand down slowly between his hands. If he senses your hand, he slowly moves both of his hands an inch or two closer together without making contact. If his hands make contact with each other or with your hand, he needs to relax and start over. With practice, some students get very good at sensing their partner's hand.

As your partner sits in a *seiza* position with his eyes closed and his hands about six inches apart, slowly move one of your hands up and down between his.

If any contact is made, the exercise must be restarted.

The second exercise involves three or four advanced students. The students stand in a circle at an arm's length apart, with one person in the middle with his eyes closed and his arms at his sides. He nods when he is relaxed, and each student slowly reaches toward his shoulders or head, one at a time in a random manner. When he senses the extended hand, he turns toward it. The students take turns being in the middle of the circle. This activity can help you significantly develop your awareness of other people's ki.

One member of the four-man team stands in the center in a ready position. When his eyes are closed and he's relaxed, he nods to signal that he's ready to begin the exercise.

The trainer slowly reaches his hand to within two or three inches of the trainee, holds it there for a moment and then slowly retracts it.

This process is repeated randomly by each trainer.

If the trainee senses a hand, he slowly turns in the direction of the attack and blocks it.

As the trainee's forearm is raised to block, the trainer retracts his hand so that no contact is made. If contact is made, the entire exercise must be repeated from the beginning.

## Visualization

The ability to visualize a situation or perceive what might happen within a given environment is a great asset that can provide tremendous benefits in the real world. The saying "keep your options open" directly applies to both martial arts training and street effectiveness. If you can picture how techniques can be carried out or what alternative techniques or courses of action are open to you, you will be better prepared to deal with real situations. For this reason, it is very important—even for new students—to practice reacting to street situations in the dojo. You will only have options if you learn to have options.

## Contemplation

An integral skill developed through meditation is contemplation—the process of exploring an idea, coming up with possible solutions or conclusions and reflecting on those solutions to decide which is best. As a martial artist, your ability to reflect on the progress of your training is critical to improving performance in your art. This will allow you to use hindsight to see what areas you need to improve and what specific skills need additional attention.

## Mushin

I tell my students, "The slowest thing you have working for you is your mouth. If you talk your way through the movements of a technique, it will be very difficult to get the technique down. The second slowest thing going for you is your mind. If you think out each move, it will still be a slow process. The best way to work through a technique is to simply let your mind guide you through it, without verbalizing or thinking about each move."

In terms of self-defense, a state of mushin is the ultimate position from which to defend yourself. Being in a state of mushin allows you to go with the flow of the situation and automatically adapt, without conscious thought or effort, to changes as they occur. When your mind is completely relaxed and receptive, your reaction time is greatly reduced and you react automatically to threats or actual physical attacks.

## Summary

There are different types of meditation: short relaxation techniques, centering (in which you attempt to connect to your inner self or hara), body awareness (which can be used to control pain in some cases), projection (which is similar to imagining) and focusing (in which you seek resolution to a problem). The time required is determined by the type of meditation you plan to practice. It can be from a few seconds to days. Everyone needs time to reflect, contemplate, reason things out and seek solutions from within.

All forms of meditation have common characteristics: improved self-confidence and sense of humility, greater awareness of your environment, improved ability to handle crises and greater objectivity—all of which have a tremendous value to the serious martial artist and development of the sixth sense. Meditation also has several goals: relaxation, visualization and contemplation—all of which are essential to success in any martial art. If your mind is in a state of mushin, it can function most effectively as no conscious thought is taking place and your mind functions automatically. In terms of the street, being in a state of mushin is the ultimate position to place yourself in terms of self-defense.

# PART III:
# HOW TO MAKE TECHNIQUES WORK

In the first part of this book, we explored the physics behind the movements of the human body that make techniques in most martial arts work. In the second part, we explored the different kinds of meditation and their essential role in martial arts training. In this section, we will put these elements together to achieve a greater understanding of what makes techniques work well. There are two concepts you need to understand in order to make techniques work better. The first is the proper way to set up and execute techniques, and the second is the value of kata.

## Muscle vs. Mass

It's not how much muscle you have; it's how you use it. I would be the last person to say that muscle has no value in the effective execution of techniques. However, excess muscle and the misuse of strength can hinder optimum movement and flexibility.

Physical strength can be an advantage as long as you are relaxed enough to sense and redirect your opponent's ki, but it can hinder the efficient use of your and your attacker's ki if you simply use brute force to cause the technique to work. Will the technique be successful? Possibly. But you'll have no real control over the technique or its outcome because you're not using ki to maximum efficiency. The blind use of strength totally negates

If you align your body so your attacker is flush against it (close enough to rotate around your y-axis), you will control his mass and your techniques will be easier to execute and more effective.

the use of proper technique. It may work in a street situation if your strength is greater than your opponent's, but it may not, and that's why the proper execution of the technique is important.

Mass, on the other hand, can be thought of as the "opposite" of muscle. When you move an object, whether by sheer muscular strength or through the use of ki, you are moving its mass. Mass is defined as "an object's inertia or resistance to movement." Mass does not equal weight; an object's weight is determined when gravitational pull is applied to its mass. Strength is not required to move your opponent's mass if you combine your ki with his and redirect his movement with the proper leverage techniques.

## Force vs. Leverage

Just as there's a difference between strength and mass, there's a difference between force and leverage. Force is defined as the amount of energy required to push or pull mass. If you want something moved in a particular direction, you must exert a certain amount of energy, either by sheer muscular strength or by leverage. If your opponent is standing still and is well balanced, it will be difficult to move him without using a great deal of force (on the assumption that you don't know any off-balancing techniques). If you're opponent is actively resisting your "moves," you will have to use far greater force to counter his resisting force just to get both of you to a neutral position. In most cases, force-vs.-force altercations do not result in a positive outcome. Even the winner will probably incur a lot of damage. Size matters in these kinds of altercations, and remember, a smaller person will probably never attack you, especially if he's alone.

The effective use of leverage can allow you to use another person's mass and force to your advantage. All the techniques in judo and aikido (including *aikijitsu* and *aikijujitsu*) are based on the use of levers to set up and execute techniques. Levers provide a means by which to use your opponent's mass or weight combined with a pivot point and your own movement to move a greater force with significantly less effort. Leverage allows you to channel your opponent's momentum in a particular direction in which you can more effectively defeat him. The ultimate advantage of leverage is that it allows a lesser force to overcome a larger force. That's why the effective use of leverage is an essential element of effective self-defense. It will give you the advantage you need to deal with a bigger assailant.

## Less Is More

When I was in my sensei's class, we joked that he weighed 120 pounds in a wet *gi*. In street clothes, he looked like a frail weakling. However, under that clothing was well-trained and well-tuned muscle. I don't think he had an ounce of fat on him. As a treat, he would occasionally bring Gene LeBell to class with him. If we were lucky, we'd be invited to throw him (easier said than done). It was like trying to throw a well-rooted tree. The upper belts were given 30 seconds or so to try and throw him using our judo knowledge, and then *"whap!"*—we'd be on the mat. He had an uncanny ability to sense what we were going to do, and he'd block or counter it. We'd be able to perform a technique on him only if it was done absolutely correctly, and then he'd go down for us.

All great sensei have something in common. They use mass, leverage and ki effectively to maximize their opponent's energy output while keeping theirs at a minimum. By remaining calm and relaxed, they can sense what their opponents are trying to do and negate or counter it. Great sensei are successful in part because they believe in the concept of "less is more." If you are physically and mentally relaxed, you'll have greater awareness or sensitivity toward what your attacker is trying to do—how his axes are interacting with your axes within their respective spheres. If you are relaxed and in a state of mushin, you can react automatically and in such an efficient manner that your energy output level (use of ki) is very low. Thus your opponents can be easily subdued with minimal effort.

"Less is more" is an important concept in any martial arts training, and it probably applies to the learning of any other skill in your life. Following this concept, the harder you try to do something, the more difficult it will be to accomplish. Accomplishment becomes more difficult because you are expending too much energy in an inefficient manner to accomplish the task. "Less is more" can lead to success in other areas beyond the martial arts—in business, sports or politics.

## Breathing

We've already dealt with breathing in the context of meditation, but we need to look at it again briefly in terms of executing techniques within a martial art. Obviously, proper breathing is essential to success in any sport. It is also an absolute necessity in terms of self-defense. From a simple psychomotor viewpoint, controlling your breathing will help control your heart rate, which will help control your emotional state, which will control the amount of adrenaline and other hormones going into your system when you're under severe stress, all of which will affect your breathing and heart rate. Keeping your breathing slow and your heart rate down will help you retain your calm and reduce your stress level. Being able to remain calm allows you to be relaxed, maximize your senses, and be more aware and in control of what is going on around you. As with the meditation process, taking a deep breath or two during a stressful event can help you center yourself and center your ki. It can also help you better handle the confrontation.

Proper breathing is essential to the efficient execution of techniques in any martial art. The basic rule is to inhale as you set up a technique and exhale as you execute it. For example, inhale as you move into a koshi nage and exhale as you actually throw your opponent, or inhale as you flex your arm and exhale as you strike.

The key to exhaling properly is to kiai as you execute the technique. Using a good kiai helps your ki flow properly. It also gets all the air out of your lungs. Holding your breath during the execution of any technique will halt the ki flow, and you will have to use more strength and effort; you will end up using muscle rather than mass and force rather than leverage. You will also dramatically reduce your chances of success in defending yourself, especially if your assailant is your size or bigger.

## The Value of Kata

If you've talked to any traditional sensei or have been in a traditional dojo, you've heard about the importance of kata. It will train your body and your mind, and it will teach you patience. But there are other, deeper reasons for learning kata.

In jujitsu, the term "kata" refers to specific techniques—such as a hip throw, wrist-lock submission, etc.—rather than to a combination of solo moves, as it does in most martial arts. Although one could go through the motions of a hip throw alone, he wouldn't really learn it without having someone to throw. That's the value of the uke. Only with a partner can you get a true feel for how the technique works when executed properly. The goal of kata practice is to ingrain moves into your mind in their ideal form so that they will be automatic and that you'll know what it feels like to properly execute a strike or a throw. In a street situation, nothing will work as perfectly as it did in class. However, if you know how a move feels when it's executed perfectly, you'll have a better chance of executing it well enough on the street to be effective.

Another aspect of self-defense is the ability to respond appropriately. To that extent, your mind has to quickly and continually assess and reassess your situation, and kata practice enables one to have techniques to draw on that are appropriate to the situation.

When teaching kata, sensei usually use large movements, which are easier for new students to interpret, learn and practice. Using large movements is also an excellent way to teach the concepts of leverage, planes and spheres, as well as the concepts and roles of ki, the saiki tanden, balance and kuzushi. However, if you walk into some jujitsu and aikido dojo, you'll notice that the higher ranks don't use large movements to execute techniques. Their techniques are not only more subtle but also more effective. Are they doing different techniques, or did something change in the instructional process?

The techniques are the same, but the instructional process is different. As students' skills improve, they are encouraged to refine their techniques and make smaller and more efficient movements. They eventually learn to bring the execution of their techniques as close as possible to their center point to create maximum effect with the least effort. This allows practitioners to maintain their center of balance and a sound base while minimizing extraneous movement. As less movement is required to execute kata, the *tori* learns that a small change in pressure can have a major effect on the uke's joint-chain hierarchy.

I call this teaching approach the "cone concept." At the base of a cone, there is a large circle. As you move up the cone, the radius becomes smaller and smaller until you reach the tip. This concept can be applied to teaching techniques; as students become more advanced, techniques are taught and executed with more efficiency and subtlety. The visible execution of a perfectly performed technique is almost impossible to detect because the movements are so small and the rotation on the y-axis is so subtle.

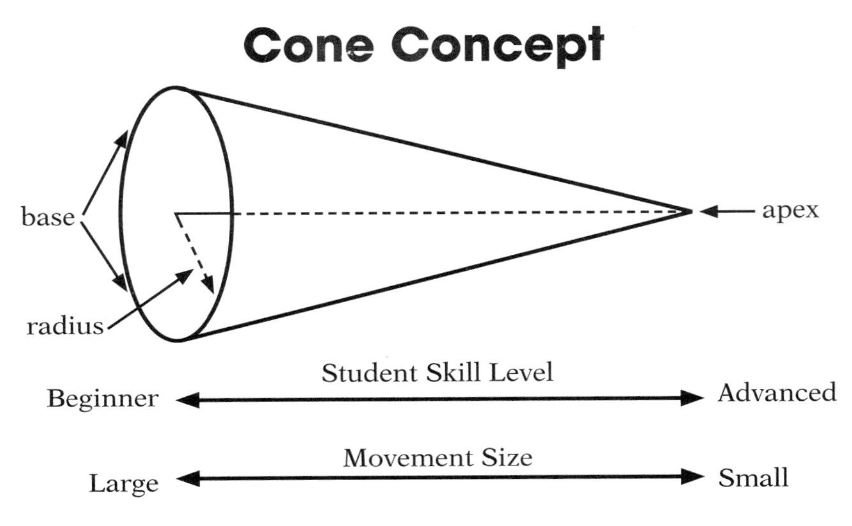

The cone concept is also a valuable way of visualizing the use of ki. Even though large movements are essential in helping students learn how to use ki, executing techniques using a smaller and smaller radius (until they reach the apex of the cone) helps students learn how to use ki efficiently. As the use of ki becomes more efficient, techniques will be executed much faster. With practice, the illusion is created that you have done "nothing" while your attacker quickly falls to the ground or flies through the air. There are no secret techniques—only skilled martial artists.

# CONCLUSIONS

Learning is a process, and true learning is an endless process involving the desire, ability and commitment toward understanding and mastery. True learning with respect to any topic, including a particular martial art, can last a lifetime. Rather than looking at your art as simply a series of moves to master, now that you've read this book, you can hopefully look at all of your acquired knowledge and realize that you've scratched the surface of understanding your art.

Hopefully, you will have a better understanding of the kinesthetics of your art, the relationship between meditation and optimum performance, and the role of *kata* in bringing these two elements together. You may also have come to realize that kata practice and self-defense skills must be a continuous part of your training regardless of rank or level of knowledge. It is these two forms of practice that bring the kinesthetic and meditative skills together to reach mastery of your art.

Perhaps, by this point, you also have realized that there are no secrets in any martial art. There are only different levels of knowledge and understanding. There is also a reality check here, in that different styles of the same art may teach specific moves and techniques in different sequences—that is to say that a move taught only to black belts in one *ryu* may be taught to beginning students in another ryu. So much for "secrets." At some point in your training, you'll realize that the more you learn, the less you know. Each door you open and enter will put you in a room with more doors to choose from.

If you plan to master a martial art, you must commit yourself to a lifetime of learning. You will continue to learn from your *sensei*. And if you have an open mind—which is an essential characteristic of being a martial artist—you also will learn from other arts.

When you become a sensei, you'll learn from your students. If you've provided your students with a sound foundation, they will find different ways to do things and put moves together. If they can do this, consider it a compliment. You've given them two tremendously valuable things: technical knowledge and the confidence to experiment with what they've learned. This should not be seen as a threat to your ryu, your art or to you. As a sensei, it is your responsibility to channel this growth so your students have a better understanding of what they are being taught. This process will validate the art for them and is one of the most important lessons they can learn.

As a responsible martial artist, you also have to have a strong philosophical base. It is important that you read and learn as much as you can about the philosophical roots behind your martial art and the martial arts in general. You also will learn from your own experiences if you take the time to reflect on what you have learned. You will develop insights into how techniques work, relationships and similarities between techniques and, surprisingly, the true value of your sensei. To make this work, you must realize that you will have plateaus in your learning—times when you think you're not learning anything or going anywhere. These plateaus will give you time to think, reflect and gain insight into what you have learned. However, if you believe in yourself and your abilities (your martial arts training will give you this confidence), you will continue to grow and develop a strong knowledge base.

You can choose to master a martial art, or you can be a martial arts practitioner—"a jack-of-all-trades and master of none"—and learn bits and pieces of a variety of arts. You might even earn black belts in two or three of them (which is commendable in and of itself). However, you will never gain true mastery of any of them.

## A Personal Note

Researching and writing this book was a tremendous learning experience for me. I learned a great deal about human kinesthetics and the relationship between meditation and the martial arts, but I still have a lot more to learn. I had some preconceptions before starting my research, some of which were validated and some of which were found to be erroneous. However, that's part of learning. If you don't pick up a few bumps and bruises on the mat, you've missed an important part of the learning process: making mistakes.

When I initially started the research for this book, I was thinking only in "*jujitsu* terms," as jujitsu is my parent art and the art I've been solely committed to teaching since 1968. However, I soon realized that such narrow thinking ignored the similarities that could be applied to many or all other martial arts. I sincerely hope I got this idea across in this book, and it will help you look at your martial art and other martial arts in a different light. Sometimes, when you're climbing the mountain, you'll find yourself taking an alternate path. That's OK, as long as you're still moving upward.

As a result of my research, I've started to find similarities in many jujitsu techniques, and this will inevitably affect how I teach my students. Yes, beginning students will still learn specific techniques and movements—they need the basics. But advanced students will now have the opportunity to learn advanced concepts that may simplify their training, help them learn faster and make them better sensei.

Will I ever be able to trim down the 800-plus techniques and variations from *budoshin* jujitsu down to 10 basic concept techniques, like professor Steve Heremia did? I don't know. I would like to believe that writing this book has started the process. With some really dedicated black belts and a lot of time, it's a possibility. If I don't do it, hopefully one or more of them will.

# GLOSSARY

# GLOSSARY

*NOTE: Entries followed by (J) indicate terminology of Japanese origin.*

**abduction:** rotation or movement of joints or extremities away from the center of the body

**adduction:** rotation or movement of joints or extremities toward the center of the body

**aikijitsu:** a type of *jujitsu* that emphasize the use of joints and joint-locking techniques (J)

**anatomically:** having to do with the placement of parts of a body, human or otherwise

**apex:** the point of a cone, where the radius from the center of the circle to the perimeter is zero (0)

**axes:** plural form of "axis"

**axis:** a straight line upon which something rotates

**balance:** physical steadiness that allows you to maintain your y-axis through your zero point

**ball-and-socket joint:** a joint in the human body where one bone fits into a "cupped" end of another bone and its end can rotate in that "cup" to a certain extent; a ball-and-socket joint is a synovial joint

**base:** the bottom or foundation of something

**cartilaginous joint:** a limited-movement joint with cartilage between the bones its connects, such as the area between your vertebrae and sacrum/hip bone

**center of balance:** zero point in your body where the x-, y- and z-axes cross (a.k.a. *saiki tanden*, *hara*, etc.)

**centering:** in meditation, the process of emptying your mind of everyday external and internal thoughts so you can balance your mind with your *hara* (or center point)

**cervical:** seven vertebrae between the skull and base of the neck, referred to as C1 to C7

**child bone:** any bone that extends from a parent bone in a straight line

**child joint:** any joint below a parent joint

**circular:** in the shape of, relating to or moving in a circle; round

**circular force:** redirecting another person's energy or force in a circular manner

**complementary force:** adding your energy to the direction of energy of your attacker; may evolve into circular force

**cone:** a geometric shape in which the circumference of a circle declines to zero along the axis of the radius

**contemplation:** to think about something carefully, usually over a long period of time

**control hold:** a joint lock that is used to control the movement and cooperation of an assailant; may also be called a "proper hold" if resistance by the assailant can lead to increased pain and eventual joint injury

**do:** way (J)

**effort:** the amount of energy or force required to move a mass a specific distance

**ellipsoidal joint:** a modified ball-and-socket joint in which the joint is elongated

**endorphin:** neurotransmitter that acts like a natural morphine receptor; the receptor is an anti-stress hormone that causes a reaction in the brain which temporarily relieves pain or induces euphoria

**environment:** all the conditions, circumstances and influences surrounding and affecting you

**euphoria:** a strong feeling of well-being, relaxation or satisfaction

**excessive force:** use of force beyond what is considered reasonable (See "reasonable force.")

**fibrous joint:** immovable joint that has no movement, such as the bones that make up the skull

**first-class lever:** a lever in which the load (L) is at one end, the fulcrum (F) is in the middle and the effort (E) is at the other end

**five senses:** the natural senses of hearing, sight, taste, smell and touch

**focusing:** the act of mentally concentrating on something

**force:** the amount of energy directed in a particular direction to move a mass a certain distance

**fulcrum:** the pivot point of a lever

**hane goshi:** inner sweeping hip throw (J)

**hara:** center or balance point of the human body; also the *saiki tanden* or zero point in an XYZ-axis (J)

**hard response:** to meet force with an equal or greater force, usually at 90 or 180 degrees to the direction of the original force

**hinge joints:** joints that have limited movement along only one plane, such as the knee, elbow, toe and finger joints

**holistic:** a level of thinking, theory or situation in which the total may or may not exceed the sum of all the parts, but within which all the elements are related to one another

**humanoid joint:** the sacrum; root joint of the human body (off-balancing this joint makes all techniques in all martial arts possible)

**impact:** to strike an object with force

**impact force:** the amount of force used to strike an object

**injury:** any cellular damage to a living body that may cause pain and inability to use that part of the body

**isometric:** a form of muscle exercise that involves simultaneous equal flexion and extension of the muscle so that the resistance to movement is the same as the pressure toward movement in the same direction and no actual physical movement takes place

**jitsu:** art (J)

**joint chain:** series of joints in the human body that are connected to one another

**joint-chain hierarchy:** the order of a joint chain from parent joint through the child joint(s)

**joint resistance/dampening:** increased inability of a joint to move in a particular direction due to the ligaments connecting the bones of the joint having reached their limit of movement

**jujitsu:** *ju* = gentle, *jitsu* = art (may be spelled in numerous other ways, along with philosophical arguments regarding the spelling and transliteration of the Japanese language) (J)

**karada makikomi:** body-winding throw (J)

**kata:** form (J)

**ki:** energy flow (J)

**kiai:** loud shout during a technique

**kinesthetics:** the interrelationship of the skeletal structure to movement of the human body

**kote gaeshi:** wrist-lock takedown (J)

**kuzushi:** the ability to maintain your balance or maintain your balance while unbalancing your opponent (J)

**levels of force:** different levels of action directed against an opponent ranging from verbal disarming through the use of deadly force

**lever:** a bar that pivots on a fulcrum and allows you to move a larger force or mass with a lesser force or mass

**leverage:** use of a lever to gain a physical advantage over the stability or balance of another object, or to move that object

**linear:** referring to a straight line or straight direction of movement

**load:** the mass of an item that is moved with a lever

**mae hiki nage:** forward pulling throw (J)

**mae yubi nage:** forward finger throw (J)

**mass:** the amount of matter in an object in a state of inertia (no movement)

**meditation:** to reflect or contemplate anything, usually in a relaxed or peaceful environment

**modality:** refers to the kind, state, status or form of something

**momentum:** mass of a body times its velocity (how fast it is moving)

**mushin:** no-mind; a condition in which no conscious mental activity is required to accomplish a task or series of tasks (J)

**opposing force:** using equal or greater force to stop/counter a force directed against you, usually at 180 degrees to the direction of the attack

**origin (origin point):** see zero point, *hara*, *saiki tanden*, etc.

**osoto gari:** outside rear sweep (J)

**pain compliance:** using a control hold or pressure point to create only enough controlled pain or discomfort to cause an attacker to physically cooperate with you

**parallel:** describes two lines that extend in the same direction and are the same distance apart at every point, so as never to meet

**parent bone:** the bone closest to the head in a joint-chain hierarchy

**parent joint:** the top joint in a joint-chain hierarchy, usually the one that is closest to the skull in humans

**perception:** how one "sees" things, based upon fact, experience, knowledge, understanding and other objective or subjective factors

**perpendicular:** positioned at a right angle (90 degrees) in relation to something

**pivot:** to rotate on an axis, keeping one part of your body as the center of the axis

**pivot joint:** a joint that rotates or pivots around an axis

**plane:** a level area within a sphere in which one of the values of x, y or z remains constant while the value of the other two fields vary

**primal:** primitive or basic

**quadrant:** any one of the eight sections that can be created from the x-, y- and z-axes; 1/8 of a sphere originating at the center and moving out to the outer edge of the sphere along the x-, y- and z-axes

**reaction gap:** the time gap—created by one or more distraction techniques—that delays an attacker's ability to respond to what you are doing

**reaction time:** amount of time it takes the human mind to recognize something has happened and direct a reaction to that event (usually 0.3 to 0.7 seconds per event)

**reasonable force:** the amount of force reasonably necessary to protect yourself from further injury and remove yourself from danger; may be determined after the fact in a court of law

**right angle:** the angle of a perpendicular structure; 90 degrees

**root joint:** the joint at the base of the skull

**rotation:** to rotate (or move around) an axis

**ryu:** style or system of a martial art (J)

**sacrum:** the five connected vertebrae that form joints with the hip bones and stabilize the pelvis

**saiki tanden:** center point of the human body, about 2 inches below the navel (See *hara*, zero point.) (J)

**second-class lever:** a lever in which the fulcrum (F) is at one end, the load (L) is in the middle and the effort (E) is at the other end

**seiza:** formal sitting position (J)

**sensei:** teacher (J)

**sixth sense:** a greater-than-normal awareness of your surroundings, particularly with regard to those elements that may affect you

**sode hiki nage:** sleeve-pulling throw (J)

**soft response:** response to an attack that may use complementary or circular force rather than opposing force

**soft techniques:** techniques that involve redirecting the energy or *ki* of an attacker and minimizing the chance of him being injured

**sphere:** a round three-dimensional object; a ball

**submission technique:** a control hold or pin designed to cause the opponent to cease fighting or suffer serious injury

**synovial joint:** joints that are freely moveable within their joint sturcture or design (Most joints in the human body are synovial.)

**tachi waza:** ready position (J)

**tatami:** mat (J)

**te nage:** hand throw (J)

**tekubi shimi waza:** wristlock (takedown) (J)

**third-class lever:** a lever in which the fulcrum (F) is at one end, the effort (E) is in the middle and the load (L) is at the other end

**tori:** person executing a technique (J)

**torque:** a force that causes rotation or something to rotate about (around) an axis

**torsion:** the actual process of twisting an object about its axis or the mechanical pressure applied to force the object to rotate on its axis

**trap:** to catch or prevent from moving away

**uchi garai:** inner rear-sweeping throw (J)

**ude guruma:** armbar (J)

**ude guruma makikomi:** armbar winding throw (J)

**ude guruma ushiro:** shoulder-lock rear takedown/throw (J)

**ude hiki no maki:** sleeve-pull winding throw (J)

**uke:** person upon whom a technique is executed (J)

**ushiro sode nage:** rear sleeve throw (J)

**Venn Diagram:** in education, business and other fields, two or more circles representing two groups (of ideas, people, things, concepts, etc.) that partially overlap each other. The area that overlaps contains similarities between the two groups. The non-overlapping areas indicate differences.

**vertebrae:** the separate bones between the skull and the pelvis that collectively compose the backbone

**weight:** measurement of the mass of an object when gravity is applied to it

**x-axis:** horizontal axis that extends out from the zero point of the y-axis, at a right angle to both the y- and z-axes

**y-axis:** vertical axis that extends perpendicularly from the zero point of the x- and z-axes

**z-axis:** horizontal axis that extends out from the zero point of the y-axis perpendicular to both the x- and y-axes (to the front and back of the y-axis when the y-axis is at rest in its natural position)

**zero point:** same as *hara, saiki tanden*

# RESOURCES FOR FURTHER STUDY

## RESOURCES FOR FURTHER STUDY

If you are interested in expanding your knowledge of any of the topics presented in this book, you are encouraged to read the books listed below:

Baggaley, Ann (editor). *Human Body*. London: Dorling Kindersley Ltd., 2001.

Cleary, Thomas. *Soul of the Samurai; Modern Translations of Three Classic Works of Zen & Bushido*. North Clarendon, VT: Tuttle Publishing, 2005.

Enoka, Roger M. *Neuromechanics of Human Movement*. 3rd ed. Champaign, IL: Human Kinetics Publishers, 2001.

Fontana, David. *Learning to Meditate*. London: Duncan Baird Publishers, 1999.

Gray, Henry. *Gray's Anatomy of the Human Body*. Philadelphia: Lea & Febiger, 1918. 20th edition, New York: Bartleby.com, 2000.

Gunaratana, Bhanta H. *Mindfulness in Plain English, Updated and Expanded Edition.* Somerville, MA: Wisdom Publications, 2002.

Harrison, Eric. *Teach Yourself to Meditate in 10 Simple Lessons*. Berkeley, CA: Ulysses Press, 2001.

Jou, Tsung Hwa. *The Tao of Meditation: Way to Enlightenment*. North Clarendon, VT: Tuttle Publishing, 1983.

Kirby, George. *Jujitsu: Basic Techniques of the Gentle Art*. Santa Clarita, CA: Ohara Publications Inc., 1983.

Kirby, George. *Jujitsu: Intermediate Techniques of the Gentle Art*. Santa Clarita, CA: Ohara Publications Inc., 1985.

Kirby, George. *Jujitsu Nerve Techniques: The Invisible Weapon of Self-Defense*. Santa Clarita, CA: Black Belt Communications LLC, 2001.

Munenori, Yagyu. (William S. Wilson, trans.). *The Life Giving Sword: Secret Teachings from the House of the Shogun*. Tokyo: Kodansha International, 2003.

Muscolino, Joseph. *Kinesiology: The Skeletal System and Muscle Function*. St. Louis: Mosby Inc., 2006.

Neumann, Donald A. *Kinesiology of the Musculoskeletal System: Foundations for Physical Rehabilitation*. St. Louis: Mosby Inc. (Elsevier), 2002.

Oatis, Carol A. *Kinesiology: The Mechanics & Pathomechanics of Human Movement*. Philadelphia: Lippincott Williams & Wilkins, 2004.

Patton, Kevin T. and Gary A. Thibodeau. *Mosby's Handbook of Anatomy & Physiology*. St. Louis: Mosby Inc. (Elsevier), 2002.

Roche, Lorin. *Meditation Made Easy*, 1st ed. New York: Harper Collins (Harper San Francisco), 1998.

Simpkins, Ph.D, C. Alexander and Annellen M. Simpkins, Ph.D. *Simple Zen; A Guide to Living Moment by Moment*. North Clarendon, VT: Tuttle Publishing, 1999.

Soho, Takuan. (William S. Wilson, trans.). *The Unfettered Mind: Writings of the Zen Master to the Sword Master*. Tokyo: Kodansha International, 1986.

Tarver, D.E. *The Way of the Living Sword: The Secret Teachings of Yagyu Munenori*. New York: iUniverse Inc., 2003.

Thera, Nyanaponika A. *The Heart of Buddhist Meditation*. York Beach, ME: Weiser Books, 1973.

# More Jujitsu Products

## SMALL-CIRCLE JUJITSU

*by Wally Jay*

Professor Wally Jay is a *Black Belt* Hall of Fame member (1969), 10th *dan* in *jujutsu* under Juan Gomez (a top disciple of Henry S. Okazaki) and a sixth dan in judo under Ken Kawachi. Jay is one of the few martial artists this century to have come up with a theory of fighting, developed it and put it into practice. His influence is felt throughout the martial arts industry.

**Volume 1** discusses the 10 basic principles of small-circle *jujutsu*, including an explanation and demonstration of finger, wrist and joint locking. (Approx. 40 min.) **DVD Code 4089—Retail $34.95**

**Volume 2** discusses in-depth advanced arm, wrist, finger and leg locks. (Approx. 40 min.) **DVD Code 4099—Retail $34.95**

**Volume 3** discusses grappling, including falling, effective throws, advanced chokes and resuscitation. (Approx. 40 min.) **DVD Code 5119—Retail $34.95**

**Volume 4** discusses the principles of learning the tendon triceps and its importance in the application of armbars and arm locks. (Approx. 50 min.) **DVD Code 7459—Retail $34.95**

**Volume 5** discusses the principles of learning highly effective finger-locking techniques for self-defense application. (Approx. 50 min.) **DVD Code 7469—Retail $34.95**

***Buy all 5 DVDs for $139.80—Code X141 • Companion book available—Code 462***

## SMALL-CIRCLE JUJITSU

*by Wally Jay*

The complete system of small-circle *jujutsu*. Fully illustrated, this book covers falling, key movements, resuscitation, all forms of joint locks, throwing techniques, chokes and self-defense applications. Wally Jay is a member of *Black Belt's* Hall of Fame. 256 pgs. (ISBN-10: 0-89750-122-5) (ISBN-13: 978-0-89750-122-4)

**Book Code 462—Retail $17.95**

***Companion DVDs available—Code 4089, 4099, 5119, 7459 & 7469***

## JIU JITSU DE BRAZIL: Extreme Leg Attacks

*by Randy Bloom*

It's grappling to the extreme as Randy Bloom shows you the Brazilian moves you need to kick some serious tail! The Pan-American International and two-time California state champion exposes the secrets behind *jujutsu* leg attacks that are applicable on the street and suitable for all levels. Learn a variety of moves, including sweeps, armbar to leg lock, judo throws to leg locks, side mounts and much more! This tape is sure to bring your grappling game to a new level! (Approx. 68 min.) **VHS Code 8980—Retail $29.95**

## BRAZILIAN JUJUTSU: Side-Mount Techniques

*by Joe Moreira with Daniel Darrow*

Describing more than 100 moves through photographic sequences and detailed captions, Brazilian-*jujutsu* fighter Joe Moreira uses his "sequential teaching" style to delineate the network of options available to combatants dealing with side-mount situations. Having trained with the likes of Reylson Gracie and Francisco Mansour in his homeland of Brazil, Moreira founded the United States Federation of Brazilian Jiu-Jitsu and 30 branches of the Joe Moreira Jiu-Jitsu de Brazil across the United States. Today, Moreira continues to be involved with events such as the Ultimate Fighting Championship and instructs mixed martial artists such as Kimo Leopoldo. Whether you are a student, teacher or simply a fan of jujutsu, this edition will serve as a comprehensive reference for side-mount moves and will instill a deeper understanding of the art's emphasis on technique rather than strength.

149 pgs. (ISBN-10: 0-89750-145-4) (ISBN-13: 978-0-89750-145-3)

**Book Code 475—Retail $12.95**

**To order, call toll-free (800) 581-5222**

**Order our extensive selection of books, videos and DVDs at www.blackbeltmag.com**

**To receive our FREE catalog, call 1-800-423-2874 ext. 10**